FAMILY BUSINESS, RISKY BUSINESS

FAMILY BUSINESS, RISKY BUSINESS

How to Make It Work

David Bork

amacom

American Management Association

This book is available at a special
discount when ordered in bulk quantities.
For information, contact Special Sales Department,
AMACOM, a division of American Management Association,
135 West 50th Street, New York, NY 10020.

223651

Library of Congress Cataloging-in-Publication Data

Bork, David.
    Family business, risky business.

    Bibliography: p.
    Includes index.
    1. Family corporations—Management. I. Title.
HD62.25.B67   1987   658'.045   86-47594
ISBN 0-8144-5878-5

Printing number

10 9 8 7 6 5 4 3 2 1

For
Sarah
and
Dan

Preface

When I began my family business consulting practice, I initially focused on correcting the obstacles that can and do arise when families work together in business. Often a family called me only after an extreme event made it apparent that difficulties could not be sorted out by the family members themselves. The family was simply too close to the problem or did not have the necessary expertise or authority to resolve it.

As I continued in my practice, it became evident to me that the positive side of family business also needed to be expressed. There is a strong popular myth that nothing "good" can come out of working with one's family. This attitude is so ingrained in the public mind by television, film, and print media that family members themselves have come to accept it. They often do not seek solutions because they do not believe any are available.

It became important to me, as a professional in the field since 1970, to correct this assumption so that the great rewards of working together as a family could be realized. These rewards include not only increased love, respect, and unity among family members but also the profits that are generated by the enterprise.

The audience for this book is both established and emerging. Many a beleaguered family business member who reads these pages will discover a way out of what he or she perceives to be an impossible set of circumstances. For some, experienced difficulties will shrink to manageable size. The members of a budding family business will learn to avoid the pitfalls of previous generations by building into their operation the techniques and attitudes that ensure smooth continuity.

Preface

It is not possible in any one book to present solutions to the myriad problems that families encounter. However, it is possible to clarify the underlying issues and create a base of understanding that will lead to creative solutions and spark new growth and unity.

There is more than theory and understanding in these pages. There are also techniques that pertain to sound business practice. These techniques are illustrated through the case study of the Harwood family—a fictional composite of the many families I have worked with. I use the Harwoods to demonstrate variations of solutions to some very difficult problems.

The main objective of a family business is the same as that of any business: generating profits. As the family focuses on that goal first and foremost, obstacles to success can be removed. Emotional growth, improved family communication, and controlled distancing of family dynamics from business practice are additional benefits of understanding the nature of the family enterprise. Family members will develop the ability to state their business views as well as to commit themselves emotionally. They will be able to say, "I think that's a poor business decision." They will be also be able to say, "I love you," "You are important to me," "I am proud of you," and "Thank you."

All this and profits too is the message of this book.

David Bork

Acknowledgments

While I take full responsibility for the content of this book as well as its omissions, I cannot say that I got to this place all by myself. Many people have directly and indirectly been of assistance. Some must be mentioned here.

In 1970, Dr. Albert M. Powell, Jr., a Maryland-based child psychiatrist, introduced me to the family systems theories of Murray Bowen. These theories were the beginning of the integrated approach to family business described in this book. I am especially indebted to Dr. Powell for suggesting that I consider systems theory as an avenue to a better understanding of families.

Dr. Thomas D. Lonner, Research/Media Associates, Anchorage, Alaska, provided significant theoretical information for the chapter on substance abuse. He helped give perspective to some of the behavioral phenomena that I observed in families.

Without the assistance of Jean Byrd in writing, rewriting, and editing, this book would probably still be in rough manuscript form. Her creative solutions helped me to clarify the presentation of complex concepts. Of special note is Jean's writing skill in building the case studies described in these pages. Her attention to detail and her understanding of the nuances of the human condition make the cases appear real, though they are, of necessity, composites of various families I have worked with.

Patricia Sheffer typed this manuscript so many times that she has committed passages to memory. Even with the word processor to assist, Pat saw more revisions than she might have wished. Throughout the process—and, in fact, for the entire five-year period of her employment with me—her high level of competence and unfailing

Acknowledgments

good nature were a breath of fresh air. With the final punctuation, she has moved on to new challenges. I wish her every success; she will be missed!

Jan Braun has seen her share of revisions too. I am grateful for her persevering against great odds when we installed more sophisticated word processing technology.

The continuous support, encouragement, and pithy advice of Dr. Albert J. Shinkel, career counselor and friend, helped me to maintain momentum on a project that seemed to be endless.

Another special word of thanks to family therapist Dr. Charles Troshinsky, who from the beginning reinforced the fact that this goal was achievable. He believed when others did not.

Last, I wish to convey the respect and admiration I hold for "my families"—the people I have served in my family business consulting practice. Together we worked, struggled, laughed, and cried as we wrestled problems to the ground, resolved them, and got on with professionalizing their enterprises. I am humbled by their confidence and trust, and inspired by their creativity and commitment to family business.

Contents

FAMILY BUSINESS, RISKY BUSINESS

1

The Roots of Family Business

From the earliest times and in almost every culture, the family business has been prominent. Enterprising fathers with large families built many commercial empires in the Old World. On the shores of the New World, one spark that drove America toward independence was the wish of the founders to develop American enterprise and keep its profits. Thus, although the spirit of free enterprise may have been born in Europe, its strongest roots were planted in the American colonies.

The Growth of American Enterprise

Many of America's founders were entrepreneurs or successors in a family business. John Hancock (1737–1793) was the adopted nephew and partner of Thomas Hancock. Their successful whalebone business grew to become a monopoly in 1766. As relations with England deteriorated, young Hancock involved himself more deeply in the struggles of the colonists to end British business and tax policies. Finally, Hancock closed his family business to become a full-time revolutionist.

Another family businessman/patriot was Paul Revere (1735–1818), who established a business in copper and metals. With his family's help, he managed both revolutionary activities *and* a prosperous firm. His business lasted through five generations of the Revere family. In 1900, it merged with two other copper manufacturers, but the family retained operating control. In 1928, during the presidency of E. H. R. Revere, another merger turned Revere Copper into Revere Copper and Brass, Inc. Revere is still a household word synonymous with a tradition of quality and excellence in copper more than two centuries long.

Colonial women, both wives and daughters, were also patriots and heads of family business. They looked upon their work largely as a matter of practical necessity, not a career, whether in support of their husbands or in their role as widow or sole family survivor.

Abigail Adams (1744–1818), the second wife of John Adams, who later became President of the United States, managed her husband's farming and business affairs. This allowed him time to devote to revolutionary activities and to the Continental Congress. Abigail wanted to become as good a "farmeress" (in her words) as John was a statesman, and she succeeded in saving him from the financial ruin that plagued many early patriots. In addition, she was knowledgeable about politics and was an advocate of women's rights. However, she could not succeed to an acknowledged position of power because of male dominance in politics and business. As a family and as a business, the Adamses excelled and passed along a tradition of public service to their successor generations.

In the period between 1830 and 1900, many of the entrepreneurs and family names that still stand for major business success emerged. The following are only a few of the industrial leaders, inventors, and businessmen of that period: Andrew Carnegie (steel); Marshall Field (retailing); Jay Gould (railroads); J. Pierpont Morgan (banking); Samuel Cunard (shipping); Charles Goodyear (originator of rubber vulcanization); Samuel F. B. Morse (telegraph); E. B. Bigelow (carpets); John Deere (farm machinery); I. M. Singer (sewing machines); Thomas Edison (light bulb, phonograph); George Eastman (camera); Cyrus McCormick (grain reaper); Henry Ford (automobile manufacturer); P. D. Armour (meat packer); E. Remington (rifles); and Alexander Graham Bell (telephone).

Notice there are no women among them. The role of women in this era was one of subservience, and women's contributions to business were often hidden behind the names of their husbands. Yet Hettie Green, the Wall Street genius, among others, deserves a prominent place, and she'll be mentioned in more detail later on in the book.

In this seventy-year period, an explosion in transportation, communications, banking, manufacturing, and retailing took place. The United States of America became the foremost business power in the world less than a century after freeing itself from colonial domination. Its citizen families, immigrants all, had established business as a key part of the American dream.

The Twentieth-Century Entrepreneur

The onset of World War I spurred corporate growth of every kind. Small family businesses invested heavily in the growing industrialism, both in credit buying and in stock purchase. The boom collapsed on Black Tuesday, October 29, 1929, inaugurating a depression era that threatened the family dream. The generation of entrepreneurs who grew up in those dark days of financial and family instability learned that economic survival depended on ingenuity, hard work, and self-sufficiency.

3

Family Business, Risky Business

During World War II, American industry entered another boom period as it moved to fulfill military and social needs. Many family businesses grew to awesome proportions and opened themselves to public trading and professional management.

Many an heir to a family business returned from the war seasoned by conflict and impressed by the efficiency of military organization. The reality of atomic power, a state of cold war, a growing nationalism in underdeveloped countries, and the emphasis on rebuilding the world trade market presented a unique set of entrepreneurial opportunities. They also gave the young businessperson a sense of urgency and a new willingness to challenge the founder's business philosophy.

Impatient with tradition, he often started his own business enterprise.* (It is this postwar generation that now heads established family businesses that are, or should be, planning for transition to successor generations.) Wartime exposure to other cultures increased the young entrepreneur's confidence, and he easily moved his family and business to any geographic area conducive to his new industry. All in all, the late 1940s and the 1950s were a challenging time for old family businesses.

In the 1960s, many young people tried to develop lives not in traditional family settings, but in communal structures of people united by mutual interests. These "families," as they liked to call themselves, banded together into communal groups to sell their crafts and skills in an emerging technological revolution driven by sophisticated computers and compounded by a flood of foreign-made products into American markets. Others formed more traditional corporations but kept them closely held.

*Male-gender words are used throughout this book for convenience only. There are and always have been women entrepreneurs, though perhaps it is only in this decade that they are getting the recognition they deserve. "He" should be taken to include "she" unless otherwise stated.

The Roots of Family Business

By the 1970s, a gradual return to traditional family business surfaced. History may show that this drive was spearheaded by women who sought through family business to resolve the conflict between commitment to family and financial survival. By 1980, the Small Business Administration reported that there were more than 13 million family-held businesses in the United States, ranging in size from the half-billion-dollar sales of the family-operated Wrigley Company (chewing gum) to small "Mom and Pop" computer businesses operated out of the home. It was estimated (*Newsweek*, December 12, 1983) that family businesses generated between 40 and 60 percent of the gross national income.

The family business has arrived in the 1980s intact, but it is bruised and scarred. Many of the attitudes and traditions that were inherited from European culture and early colonial America are now giving rise to issues that need to be resolved if family enterprise is to continue as a vital part of American business. Succession by the oldest son, women as business inferiors, toleration of substance abuse, treatment of in-laws as outlaws, and running the business the way father runs the family—all these attitudes must give way. And they are giving way.

The Future of Family Business

The stereotype of the family business as a cauldron of unresolved personal tension and eccentric behavior is yielding to a new image in the 1980s. Newspapers and popular magazines are featuring articles on families who chose to go into business together. Many of these families will not fall into the traps that previous family businesses fell into. Better educational opportunities, increased sexual equality in the job market, and enlightened social conditions that allow families to seek help for their business problems are paving the way for a professional business atmosphere and increased communication among family members who work together.

Family business success stories are continually cropping up in the news. In New York City, three family businesses came to the attention of a *New York Times* writer in 1983. The Hazen family, which founded and runs Lloyd's Sportswear Company, generates about $25 million in annual sales from its clothing. Three sons are involved in the business, and the 77-year-old family patriarch, Freddie Hazen, calls them "a blessing." Anne Dee Goldin, senior vice president of Goldin-Feldman International, speaks of her pride in her family and of her father's happiness to see her come into the $12 million business. The sons and grandsons of Leo Honig, founder of Anglo Fabrics Company, a wool fabrics manufacturer, gravitated to the company because of the way they were taught to think about the family business. In a company that employs more than 600 people, each family member has a job that suits his talents. Also, the heirs are groomed to take over management positions because the company has a *stated goal* of continuation as a family business.[1]

In the Washington, D.C., suburb of Kensington, Dr. Leslie Grant works in association with her father, Dr. Alan Grant. The Grants, both optometrists, each see up to 30 patients every business day. They also collaborate on research and have jointly published two professional papers. Leslie's father did not encourage her early interest in optometry for fear he would unduly influence her career decision. But he helped her all he could and invited her into his practice after she graduated from the Pennsylvania College of Optometry in 1980. He treats her as a professional equal, but also plays a fatherly role when he advises her not to drive on certain icy mornings or wipes the snow off her car at the end of a business day. Leslie considers her family partnership as the best of both worlds.[2]

John Kent Cooke is the executive vice president of Pro Football, Inc., which owns the Washington Redskins. His

6

father, Jack Kent Cooke, was cited by *Forbes* magazine as one of the 400 wealthiest people in America. Cooke, Sr., whose sports franchises have included a minor league baseball club in Canada, the Los Angeles Lakers basketball team, and the Los Angeles Kings hockey team, says he is pushing himself out of the Redskins operation in favor of his son, who presently handles 50 percent of the supervisory and management tasks. The younger Cooke says that being in business with his father is like learning painting from an Old Master. The lessons are not without difficulty sometimes, but John Kent Cooke considers himself lucky: He is doing what he wants while learning from a person for whom he has great respect and admiration.[3]

In Austin, Texas, the four young Walsh brothers came together to develop a new concept in laundromats. Called "Barwash," the concept features a restaurant bar for patrons who are doing their laundry. Sandwiches, gourmet treats, television, and beer are served, and a game area is provided for children. The business was financed by their father, who is called "Deep Pockets" by his sons. The Walsh brothers hope to franchise the concept nationwide after they perfect the Austin operation. This family is representative of the many young people who enjoy working together and are increasingly choosing to do so in a family atmosphere.[4]

As Calvin Coolidge said, "The business of America is business." And the family enterprise is its backbone. Socially and culturally, the family business offers the opportunity to unify work and family concerns for the benefit of succeeding generations. In the family business lies much of the real history of America's past.

2

A Family System at Work

For the purpose of demonstrating the problems that arise in a family business and the theories and techniques used to solve them, I have created a composite fictional family. In real life, a family company will not have all the problems of this imagined enterprise—usually only one or a few. I have simply condensed all the problems so you can see the possibilities. The Harwoods, whom you are about to meet, have a very complex set of circumstances. Fortunately, they are willing to confront their problems and seek solutions.

Birth of a Dynasty

Harwood Engine and Cable, Inc. is a slightly misleading name. Its $75 million annual gross sales are derived from the manufacture of a small electrical device essential to the continuous and smooth rotation of airplane engines. The company employs 250 people in a city of 60,000. It is the largest of a small group of manufacturing concerns in a predominately agricultural area. The company enjoys an excellent national and local reputation, both in its product and in its employee relations. Harwood E&C, as it is familiarly known, is an active supporter of community endeavors. Although it began operations as recently as 1942, the company is so firmly ingrained in the community fabric that no one could imagine the town without it.

The product, a small, intricately designed system of wires and metal triggers in a compact unit, became essential during World War II to the operating precision of military aircraft. In the industry, it was considered the equal of complex computer-run systems. The mechanism had been designed by Charles Harwood, the only sibling of the current president, Louis Harwood. Charles was creative and innovative, but he had little inclination toward business. Louis, however, loved the challenge of creating a new company. He delighted in the opportunity to market his younger brother's invention and to help the national war effort at the same time. Under Louis's bold decisions and management, the company prospered, quickly bolstered by military contracts. Its growth continued throughout the 1950s and 1960s, but the onset of the jet age and imported computer systems caused its gross sales to level out by the 1980s. The company was in no danger of failing, but it was in a mature market. It needed changes in its sales approach and an updating of its manufacturing methods to keep abreast of rising costs. In addition, new opportunities for related products and foreign sales were developing.

While all this was happening, a problem arose that made business decisions of secondary importance. Louis Harwood, president and chairman of the board, was suffering from high blood pressure. Medication seemed unable to control it. His wife, Lillian, unable to keep him from working or to get him to face the seriousness of his medical condition, decided to seek outside help.

Primarily, Lillian felt her husband needed to think about a successor. Neither of their two sons—Charles and Louis, Jr.— was ready or willing to take over the business. In the event of her husband's death or incapacitation due to a prolonged illness, Lillian would be faced with selling the business they had so carefully nurtured over more than a quarter of a century. She had read about my services as a family business professional and called me to say that the family needed help.

The Surface Problem

I met first with Louis Harwood, Sr. He listed his chief concerns as the necessity to streamline operations, to expand the product line, and to enter the international market. Finding a successor was important, but it was not *his* top priority. Sixty-four years had not slowed his step, but his medical problems had dulled his enthusiasm. Business travel and long, three-martini lunches with clients, which he had once enjoyed, made him unusually tired. He had become increasingly short-tempered at the office and at home. This had prompted Lillian's insistence that he have a thorough physical examination.

At first, the knowledge of his high blood pressure did not bother him. When medication failed to keep it in check, he began to fear a major health setback that would remove him from the business. Since he viewed the company as an extension of himself, he did not see how it could go on for any extended time without him. Louis consoled himself with the notion that rest would solve his physical problem and he planned to take a two-month leave of absence. His son Charles

11

would handle the daily operation of the business during that brief period of time. Major decisions regarding future expansion could wait until his return.

Louis was somewhat annoyed by Lillian's insistence on calling in an outside consultant to look at what he saw as a manageable—and temporary—problem. But Lillian Harwood had always given her husband good advice, and his acceptance of her suggestion was supported by his unspoken anxiety about his health.

The Family Background

Louis and Lillian had married in 1945, a few years after she finished college with a degree in art history. One of her dreams had been to see the great art collections of the world, but she settled in those late wartime years for a tour of the major museums in the United States and Canada. When they first met, Louis admired Lillian's courage to travel alone and her determination to pursue her dreams. Their marriage had been fulfilling for both of them, and she proudly accepted her role as the wife of a prosperous businessman and community leader. Together they had three children. The oldest, Elaine, was the head of her own successful interior design business. The two younger children, Charles and Louis, Jr., had followed in the footsteps of their father and entered the family business.

Louis, Sr. considered his wife to be a thoughtful, attractive, well-educated woman who rarely involved herself in the "business end" of the business. When she did, he found her observations to be astute. Louis benefited from her comments and was proud of her intelligence. She was a good listener and encouraged him to share his thoughts and feelings with her as she did with him. Her unfailing loyalty and trust, plus her sense of reality, gave her opinions a perspective he needed. Louis secretly marveled at her business acumen and the organizational talents she exhibited in managing their family life and myriad community endeavors.

Lillian's natural family ties were important to her. Her older brother, John Simpson, was a successful businessman in a nearby city. She was close to her brother, who, like her husband, held her in considerable esteem. Lillian balanced her family commitment with love and skill.

Charles, her brother-in-law, enjoyed having her in the family. He took advantage of Lillian's willingness to listen and poured out a constant stream of ideas for inventions. He did not marry, preferring to tinker with his inventions rather than make new friends. As time went on, he became more and more eccentric. He would hastily leave the dinner table at a party to write down a new idea that had popped into his mind. Then, just before his thirtieth birthday, Charles had a fatal heart attack.

Louis's grief at the loss of his brother and best friend was purged to a great extent by excessive work and a renewed commitment to the success of the Harwood business. A twelve-hour day was normal for him, but in the first years following Charles's death, he pushed himself to capacity. As his efforts produced rapid growth and prosperity for the company, he became possessive of all decisions concerning the business and involved himself in every department. In Louis's thinking, he *was* Harwood Engine and Cable, Inc. Like most entrepreneurs, he felt he would live forever and the business would always have him at its helm. Thus, the question of a successor was never given serious consideration.

In her personal interview, Lillian Harwood was clearly worried about her husband's health. From time to time, she and Louis had talked about his retirement, but he never made any plans to effect it. Now that he was forced to think of such a step, she said, he could not envision the business without him. Yet in his present state of health, she knew it would be disastrous for him to continue at his current pace. At sixty-two,

Lillian still wanted to do many things in life, and her husband was integral to most of them.

As a practical person, Lillian had to face the idea of Louis's death or a debilitating illness. She knew there would be business decisions she did not feel qualified to make. Could the children help? Lillian did not challenge her husband's view that his only possible successor was their son Charles. However, unknown to his father, Charles had confided in Lillian that he wanted out of the business. Louis, Jr., the youngest of the three children, did not appear ambitious to manage the firm. Lillian thought Elaine, the oldest child, had the ability to manage the company, as demonstrated by her own successful business. It was, therefore, a shock to Lillian when Elaine turned down her mother's request to attend Harwood board meetings. Puzzled and hurt by Elaine's unexplained refusal, Lillian concluded that the only option would be to sell the company if Louis's health continued to deteriorate. This thought saddened her. The company had become an integral part of her life, and she did not want to give up what the Harwood family had so earnestly built.

The Harwood Sons: Real Feelings Emerge

In the personal interviews with the two sons, another picture began to emerge. Son Charles was assistant to the president, but without portfolio. During his session with me, Charles was edgy. He chain-smoked and was obviously anxious to have the meeting end. He had arrived late and his appearance, especially in contrast to that of the other family members, was too casual. His look was one not of artistic dishevelment, but of simple neglect.

In discussing his father's health and its impact on the business, Charles said it was obvious that the family should sell. No one, he explained, except his father, was really interested in or capable of running the firm. Charles acknowledged that he wanted to leave his position. He said his father's long "briefings" about details were annoying. Further, he did not enjoy business on a day-to-day basis. The family had "expected" Charles to join the company after college, and so he had. He admitted his knowledge of the business made him a valuable asset to his father. Louis, Sr. bounced his thinking off his oldest son, but rarely took or credited his advice. Recently, Louis had begun to interpret Charles's increasing reticence as approval of the older man's decisions.

Charles John Harwood had been named for his two uncles. From the time he was born, he was the apple of his father's eye. Louis took him everywhere, including occasional visits to the office. His role as sidekick and confidant to his father grew even stronger after he joined the firm in 1970. Now, he found himself torn between loyalty to his father and his own needs, which were becoming more difficult to meet. He was unmarried at thirty-six, and still uncertain about his life goals.

Like his namesake uncle, Charles was creative. In college, he had majored in business, but found time to take drama courses, which he loved. His community could always count on him to support music, art, and theater. Charles's efforts to raise funds for a new fine arts center were immensely successful, and a source of pride to his parents.

As a child, Charles remembered his father as an authoritative yet loving person. His mother supported his father's decisions regarding the children wholeheartedly, but she was always available to Charles for special confidences or to work out solutions to difficult problems.

Charles was painfully aware that his brother and sister had been envious as children of his special bond with their father. Their attempts at excellence in school and sports were largely to capture a part of the attention Louis, Sr. lavished on his first son. However, the more Elaine and Louis, Jr. succeeded, the more their father prodded them to new successes. They never gained the measure of quiet acceptance Charles received regardless of his efforts. On his part, Charles felt emotionally separated from his siblings.

Personal discussion of his family made Charles uncomfortable. He attempted to cut the interview short by saying he was anxious to have lunch, although it was only 11:00 A.M. He implied a drink would also be desirable. Charles's personal appearance indicated the outward signs of alcohol abuse and serious depression. In college, he had developed a substance abuse problem. His father attributed his son's constant drinking and occasional indulgence in marijuana during that period to a "stage Charles would grow out of." Unfortunately, the problem became more severe as Charles grew older. Sometimes he came to the office late and had noticeably been drinking. However, as long as he showed up, Louis, Sr. ignored the obvious symptoms his son displayed and never referred to them.

In contrast with Charles, Louis, Jr. was a breath of fresh air. A vibrant, healthy-looking man of thirty-three, he cheerfully described his role in the company as the head of a section of the manufacturing process. Lou, as he preferred to be called, obviously loved his work and was genuinely proud of the family business and its product. The possibility of a management turnover or sale of the company because of his father's failing health was of extreme concern to him. He enthusiastically described the firm as on the verge of expansion into additional products and foreign markets. Lou felt this meant considerable growth potential.

Except to refer to Charles as "having all of father's answers," Lou offered no solution to the Harwood management succession problem. He did mention Elaine's executive ability and seemed truly proud of her, but he did not seriously consider the possibility of having her in the business. "Father," he said, "would never go for that. It's not a woman's type of business."

Lou had graduated from college with a degree in engineering, and joined "the business." He demonstrated considerable skill and interest in the firm's manufacturing processes. His father had acknowledged Lou's ability as a troubleshooter but had ignored him in administrative, marketing, or financial matters.

What did concern Louis, Sr. was his younger son's personality. Lou was respected by his co-workers and the employees of his section for his knowledge and efficiency, and for his unfailing good nature. But his father saw Lou's easygoing manner as a detriment to good management rather than as an effective style that got results. Several years after joining the firm, Lou had accepted his father's image of him as "happy go lucky" and no longer pushed himself to his full potential. He gave the business what was expected and what his father would accept, but never as much as he really wanted.

In contrast to his older brother, Lou had a solid personal and family life. He had met his wife, Joan, in college, and they married the year after graduation. Two years later their daughter, Louise, was born.

As a hobby, Lou and Joan designed mathematical skill games, which despite the urgings of their friends, they never attempted to market. True to the Harwood tradition, they were community activists and extremely well liked individuals. Lou taught an engineering course at the local junior college, and Joan gave a remedial math lab for teenagers at the high school.

An interesting sidelight that came out in Lou's interview was the relationship he enjoyed with his immediate boss, William (Bill) Archer. Bill had been hired by the Harwood brothers during the first year of the company's existence. His skill, capacity to work, intelligence, and devotion to the firm carried him upward from foreman to his post as production manager.

Bill was a year older than Louis, Sr. and looked forward to his retirement in the near future. He saw Lou as his natural successor, but the young man's lack of initiative worried Bill. In

17

an effort to spark Lou's interest, Bill gave him valuable information about the company's current manufacturing capabilities and the probable impact of future expansion plans. From Bill, Lou received the acceptance and pointed attention he never got from his father. The two men worked well together and were personal friends outside the company.

The Founder's Daughter

After the interviews with the four family members involved in the business, I was intrigued by everyone's reference to Elaine as a successful businesswoman and a capable manager. Her unwillingness to help her family in a time of business crisis seemed peculiar. I asked to interview Elaine. At first reluctant, she finally consented.

During our first interview, Elaine exuded confidence and strong leadership qualities. Her reluctance to come to the Harwood board meetings, she stated, was in deference to her father, who felt the manufacturing industry was not suitable for a woman. Elaine said this with a smile, but her voice seemed to carry a bitterness. Was she angry about her father's attitude? She agreed she was, but it was more than that. Elaine had tried hard to demonstrate to her father that she had the ability to come into the business. She had worked there part time during her high school years and college summers. In college, she majored in business and interior design, a combination that puzzled but pleased her father. Despite her grasp of business intricacies, and her thorough understanding of marketing techniques and procedures, her father had brushed off her request to take on additional responsibilities within the family company.

"He never took me seriously," she said. "It was frustrating because there was nothing I could do to convince him I was actually good at what he considered a man's job. Now he's ill and mother's afraid for some reason that the family business is going to slip away. So she asked me to come to board meetings! She never supported me for a job in the firm. Why should I become involved now? I have my own business to consider, and Charles is obviously my father's successor!"

Elaine told me about her prosperous firm—Harwood Designs International. The idea for it came to her while she was in college. After graduation, she moved to a large Midwestern city and opened an interior design company. She capitalized the effort from a trust left by her uncle Charles. At first, she subcontracted private home interiors for architects. Her ability to stay current with fashion while developing timeless interiors made her a much publicized designer sought after by wealthy clients. The husband of one such client asked her to create an interior for his corporate headquarters. He wanted an environment that would project the company's image and philosophy to clients and employees alike. The success of this project could be clearly measured by the large number of requests she received from other corporations. She added a corporate design division to her prospering home interior company. In five years, it was the larger of the two divisions.

At the time Louis, Sr.'s health deteriorated, Elaine's firm had reached its highest level of prosperity. Harwood Designs International had $15 million in annual sales. The corporate design division had offices in Atlanta, San Francisco, Houston, and London; the home interior division had branches in Dallas and Los Angeles. Both divisions were in Washington, D.C. Elaine's wealthy clientele included oil magnates, members of the jet set, politicians, and movie stars.

In the midst of this success, Elaine, at thirty-eight, was restless. She loved her business, but missed the challenge it had presented in its early years. Several options offered themselves. One was to turn the operation completely over to one of her talented managers. Another was to franchise. The final option was to sell the company. It would bring her enormous profit and allow her to start up a new idea. The problem was, she did not have a new vision on the horizon.

As the extent of her father's health problem became known to her, she was confused about a decision concerning her future at Harwood E&C. Elaine understood the necessity for expanding her knowledge of the family business, but she saw herself only in a consulting position, perhaps reviewing the company's financial situation. She was reluctant to appear aggressive in her father's eyes, especially in an area he considered off-bounds to her. She feared her anger and frustration would eventually surface and would make the present situation worse. She loved her parents, and had accepted her father's attitudes, but she could not live with them at close hand. For this reason, she had grown somewhat distant from the family, especially when it became apparent that the time was approaching for her father to choose his successor. She felt if she was not involved in the business at all she would not be further angered by his decision to give the business to his sons.

Elaine's personal life revolved around her son, Kellen, and her daughter, Allison. Her seven-year marriage to Robert Colwell had ended in divorce. When Elaine married Robert, a manufacturer's representative, during the fledgling years of her company, her father hoped she would give up her business ambitions and devote herself to raising a family. She combined both. Elaine truly enjoyed her growing firm, and applied her superior organizational skills to meeting the business and family needs.

Robert felt competitive with her, and refused to take part in her business operation. He had never been invited to join the Harwood family business, despite his considerable talent and success in marketing products in related fields. Louis, Sr. felt Robert was "not good enough" to become an integral part of the operation, although the move might bring his daughter back to her home town.

When they married, Robert had an alcohol problem that

Elaine overlooked. Her father drank with his business clients and was never strict about alcohol consumption. On her part, Elaine had become health-conscious and limited her alcohol intake to social or business occasions. This, too, became a barrier in their marriage. Robert's alcohol abuse finally escalated to a point where treatment was imperative to his health and safety. He refused all offers of help, and Elaine, in desperation, divorced him. Her father had never approved of divorce, but Robert's open problem and its effects on Elaine and her two children made Louis, Sr. accept her decision. Elaine was grateful for the emotional support and encouragement he gave her during the lengthy, messy divorce proceedings. This new rapport between father and daughter deteriorated quickly as Louis, Sr. turned his full attention back to his business after the divorce was final. "It was," Elaine sighed, "business as usual."

Summary of the Harwoods' Circumstances

The Harwood family had fallen into traps very common to family enterprise. At the business level, the company had to make crucial decisions about expansion, overseas markets, additions to the product line, and/or acquisition of a related company. At the personal level, an entrepreneurial father, the question of succession, a capable but overlooked child, sibling rivalry, substance abuse—these issues stood in the way of quick and ready solutions when the family tried to deal with the possible business consequences of Louis, Sr.'s ill health.

How does a family disentangle itself from a web of past conclusions that now stand in the way of family unity? It takes work, understanding, and time. In our imaginary case, the Harwoods agreed to make the effort.

3
Family Systems Theories

Family businesses are different from other forms of enterprise. Since the fact is not generally understood, both the terms and the dynamics need to be clarified. The theories outlined here will help put the Harwood case into a systems perspective. Only when families are viewed as a system—not as a set of individual people—can problems be understood and change accomplished.

Defining a Family Business

The general public is often confused about the terms "family business" and "closely held corporation." The latter is a legal term meaning a company that has a limited number of owners and is not publicly traded. Family-owned corporations fit into this category along with other businesses controlled by a few people who may or may not be related.

Strictly speaking, a family business is one that has been started by a family member and has been passed, or is expected to be passed, to succeeding generations of the family, sometimes through marriage. Descendants of the original founder(s) will own and control the business. Also, members of the family work, participate in, and benefit from the enterprise. A family member is defined as anyone related to the family, by birth or marriage, or anyone related to the officers of the company.

The legal form of ownership has nothing to do with the scope of the enterprise. Many people hear the term "family business" and immediately think of the neighborhood Mom and Pop operation. In some cases, this is correct. At the same time, many of the largest corporations in the world are owned by single families.

The dynamics of a family that works together in a profit-making enterprise are complicated. Neither pure business techniques nor organizational theory address the dynamics fully. My own early experience is a case in point.

In 1970 I was engaged by a family corporation to assist in developing a long-term plan. The stated concern was to merge three operating entities. The companies were owned and operated by five relatives (through birth or marriage), with the assistance of two trusted employees. Although the stated purpose was to develop long-range goals for the newly merged companies, it soon became clear that the real issues were control and influence.

I dealt with the case using the state-of-the-art organizational theory then available. We moved systematically through all the professed and implied issues, developed a viable solution, and laid a solid foundation for the prosperous years that followed. Even so, I came away from the successful engagement perplexed about many of the dynamics existing among the five principals involved. It was then I had my first inkling that family-controlled enterprises might be different. If I had invited those five people to cocktails and dinner, the social dynamics would have been complicated. To have them in business together was complex.

Because I did not understand all the interpersonal dynamics functioning in the system, I began to seek a body of knowledge that adequately explained the psychosocial energies that exist in interactions among closely related people and/or people who have a long history of working together. Had it not been for that one engagement in 1970, I probably would never have explored various disciplines or developed the techniques discussed in this book.

A Family Is a System

When a family finds itself in trouble, its members rarely look to themselves as a unit to find the remedy. The family simply blames one individual who exhibits behavior that goes against the family's rules—which may or may not conform to society's rules. This is an effective way to keep the other family members from accepting part of the problem. It is *not* an effective way to remedy family problems. Experts who have worked with families over the last few decades have found that the most effective long-term treatment of family problems is a systems approach.

This approach is based on the premise that we repeat what we came out of, that we are who we are because of our family system. Each generation in a family repeats the patterns of the preceding generation. Such a theory diffuses blame backward over the generations, through the parents, grandparents, great-grandparents, and so on. It says none of us asked to be who we are. We did not write our own specifications. We merely evolved as unwittingly as our parents before us, and their parents before them.

A systems concept sees what is going on in the individual as inseparable from the family network of relationships in which the individual is embedded, the emotional processes in that system, and the way the system was balanced before symptoms appeared. It encompasses multigenerational patterns and processes. A situation in the nuclear family cannot be understood without knowing "the emotional baggage" that a husband and wife brought from their families of origin.

Discussion of family systems starts with Sigmund Freud (1856–1939), the Austrian neurologist and founder of psychoanalysis. He focused on the individual and his treatment model was one to one, patient to therapist. Freud laid many cornerstones in the understanding of human behavior. However, in the twentieth century some psychoanalysts found Freud's model lacking, particularly in dealing with severe emotional problems.

One of those psychoanalysts was Dr. Murray Bowen. He was first trained in the sciences, then in medicine, and finally in psychoanalysis. From 1946 to 1954, Bowen worked at the Menninger Clinic, where he began to treat schizophrenics. In 1959, he moved to the National Institute of Mental Health (NIMH), where he continued his studies.

Bowen found that when treated on an individual basis, the schizophrenic could make some progress, but when the patient returned to the family unit, the schizophrenic behavior returned, sometimes more pronounced. He came to believe that something occurs in the schizophrenic's family that either relates to or precipitates the schizophrenic behavior.

This finding caused Bowen to break from the orientation of Freud, which considered family members individually. Bowen began to look at the family as a *system*, and to view the patient as a component of that system. This was the first step toward the development of the Bowen family systems theory.[1]

Looking at the individual in the context of the whole family is analogous to looking at the forest instead of one individual tree. The view is telescopic, not microscopic, as shown in Figure 1. This seemingly simple departure from the historical way of looking at members of a family opens up an entirely new approach to working with families as a system.

How the System Functions

In the sciences, a system is defined as having clearly delineated boundaries with identifiable components. It is simple to deter-

Figure 1. Individual versus systems view of the family.

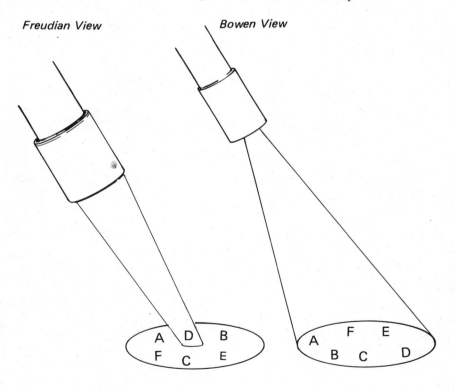

Freudian View

Bowen View

mine whether an element is in or out of a system simply by establishing where that element is with respect to the system boundaries. A family system includes not only the husband and wife and their children, but the preceding generations of each branch of the family. We begin by looking at the nuclear family, then work back through the generations. Historians tell us the past is but a prologue to the present. The Old Testament tells us who begat whom. The familiar phrase "Apples don't fall far from the tree" tells us children are like their parents. Thus, Bowen was on solid ground, historically and culturally, in viewing a family back through its generations in order to see the total family system.

There are rules that dictate how a system will function. Think of the planets in our solar system and their various satellites. These objects move with predictable regularity. Simultaneously, all the planets in the system revolve around the sun. Astronomers have complex mathematical formulas for describing the relationships among planets and their interactions. They can also calculate that a planet *should* exist in a particular position, as they did with Pluto, long before it was located by telescope.

An individual planet can be thought of as the nuclear family, the solar system as the generations that preceded, and the entire Milky Way galaxy as all humankind. The family genogram, which we will examine later, maps the family system in the same way that astronomers chart the solar system.

As surely as there are delineated rules for how the solar system functions, so there are clear rules and expectations for behavior within a family. It is no coincidence that some families devote themselves to public service or business or medicine for generation after generation. The multigenerational process conveys a range of expectations, including emotional functioning and occupational choices. Central to using family systems theory in the family business is understanding the messages carried in the family and how these messages affect the business operation.

Every human being, regardless of background, has the ability to learn, adapt, and create—to absorb new information, integrate it with material already learned, and apply it in a manner different from its original use. In this part of his theory, Bowen acknowledges that people can learn to function in ways completely different from the methods used in the family of origin. A person can exercise free will and thus depart from the expectations or messages that were handed down within the family.

At the same time, "in the clutch"—when they are under stress or pressure—people revert to the family base of functioning. This return to messages (behaviors) from the family of origin can be avoided only if the person learns how to circumvent the signals that trigger the reversion.

Let us summarize Bowen's theory to this point:

1. A family is a system.
2. Systems transmit rules, messages, patterns, or expectations for behavior.
3. We can, and do, learn behaviors different from our family messages.
4. When the pressure is on, we will revert to the pattern of our family systems unless we learn to short-circuit that reversion and behave according to patterns learned elsewhere.

Emotion versus Thought

Bowen further generalized that a range of behaviors operate in the family system, some behaviors based on emotion and some on thought. To be drawn back or to revert to the family message system is to function from an emotional base. To elect behaviors other than the deleterious ones of the family system is to operate from a thinking base.

This principle is central to the application of the Bowen family systems theory to family businesses. Some families send prevailing messages that are contradictory to, or in conflict with, sound business practices. It is, therefore, conceivable that a family could learn to operate a business effectively, but revert to its old, counterproductive style when under pressure or stress. Recognizing that some of the behavior in the family system may be incompatible with sound business practice is the unique aspect of the integrated approach to families in business.

According to Bowen, a person is programmed from birth to serve a specific set of functions, and the person "senses" what is expected from the way the system functions around him. These expectations have more impact than any verbal messages permitting the person to do as he pleases. An example is the family care giver. Often this is the person who attends to the family and aging parents. On examination we find that person has been cast in the role since childhood. Everyone has a different capacity for handling impulses as well as a limited band of choice in rejecting or transmitting the incoming data. The person's "intellectual awareness" that such a system is operating is also a factor.

Each family member, according to Bowen, becomes aware of his dependence on others in the system. Consequently, there is a wide range of "subtle alliances" for helping, refusing help, or hurting others. Several members together can punish a single member, and a single family member who is in a key position can hurt the entire family.

One predictable family pattern is placing blame for failure to function as expected. This pattern includes blaming others as well as oneself. In a tense situation, most people will place blame outside themselves or within themselves or even switch between the two. This pattern is a result of cause-and-effect thinking. However, if the head of a family remains calm in a tense situation, the entire family can be calm and the system will operate smoothly. If the key family member panics, the panic message is transmitted throughout the family system, which returns a panic message to the key member. During this cycle, messages are handled poorly, if not partially or completely distorted, and the result is paralysis of the entire system. The system can recover from an occasional panic or overload, but if the situation becomes chronic, one or more members may collapse by becoming ill.

Differentiation of Self, Triangles, and Cutoff

Differentiation of self is a cornerstone of family systems theory. Differentiation relates to how a person's emotions and intellect balance. It affects how the person functions, how a family functions, and how the person functions in relation to the family.

In the evolutionary process, the human emotional system developed earlier than the intellectual system. Simply stated, we could grunt and groan long before we had the capacity to reason. In Bowen's view, the emotional system is intuitive and operates automatically; the intellectual system is a function of the highly developed cerebral cortex. The feeling system is a bridge between the emotional and the intellectual systems by which subjective states are registered in the cortex. Accordingly, in Bowen's view, more of an individual's life is governed by automatic emotional impulse than is easily admitted.

Differentiation is the process whereby the intellect can function *separately* from the emotional system under periods of stress. It delineates the individual's self-boundaries and separates one person from another emotionally. The term "defining a self" is synonymous with differentiation.

Differentiation allows people to enter into intense relationships without a fusion of "selves." There must always be a space between "selves." When this space narrows, people suffer loss of self. They become vulnerable to stress by heavily investing themselves in the continuous borrowing and lending of self in order to maintain self.

The differentiated person is one who:

1. Has an openness about the self.
2. Has the ability to listen to others.
3. Has the ability to laugh at the self.
4. Has a willingness and enthusiasm for taking risks.
5. Focuses on solutions and options.
6. Concentrates on living in the here and now.
7. Has the ability to enter into intense relationships without loss of self.
8. Cultivates high expectations of self.
9. Enjoys close physical contact with others.
10. Organizes questions into self-statements.
11. Seeks unrestricted awareness and acceptance of all parts of the self.
12. Depersonalizes stress through taking an overview.
13. Avoids efforts to change others for any reason.

(For students of psychology, Bowen's differentiation of self and Carl Jung's individuation are one and the same.)

When anxiety builds up in people or organizations, it pours over into other relationships. Two people can manage only so much anxiety. Enter a third person to whom the anxiety can be shifted. This does not resolve issues, but it does slough off anxiety by involving another in the issue. With the involvement of the third person, the system is temporarily stabilized.

Bowen calls this predictable emotional pattern between three people *triangling*. As the smallest stable emotional unit, the triangle is considered the molecule of emotional systems. Triangling is particularly visible during times of high anxiety, but it is in operation all the time.

A key factor that affects the level of stress in a triangle, and thus in a relationship, is the level of differentiation of each member. The less well-differentiated people are, the more likely they are to become very upset and to have their emotions flood their thoughts and impair their ability to think clearly through situations.

Families often try to resolve difficulties in the midst of a system full of triangles. Rather than dealing directly with the conflict, the person goes to a third party in the system for support or reassurance. Only when triangles are eliminated can two people resolve their conflict with each other. The unfortunate fact, however, is that many people are unwilling to accept their responsibility in the conflict, and when that is the case, all the coming together with the other person is futile. The relationship between A and B will tolerate only so much tension. In this example B will attempt to drain off some pressure to C. If C is well differentiated, he will say, "I understand, but you need to take this to A" (see Figure 2a). If C is not well differentiated, he will absorb the A–B tension and return it to A (see Figure 2b). In Figure 2a, C is well differentiated; in Figure 2b, C is poorly differentiated.

The family emotional system is also governed by the degree of emotional *cutoff* with families of origin. Cutoff relates to *unresolved emotional attachment to parents*. Bowen believes that this attachment is much stronger than people would like to believe. The most typical way to handle this is to create a partial cutoff by living away from the family of origin and maintaining minimal contact with the parents. When people create a complete break—thinking they are destroying the attachment—the denied emotional attachment to the family repeats itself in the families such people create. Over time the problem becomes manifest as an emotional distance between

Figure 2. The concept of differentiation.

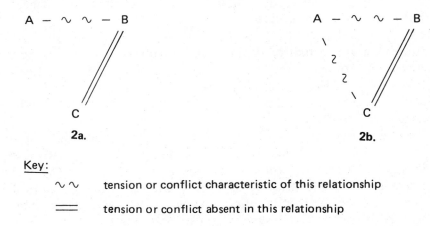

spouses, as physical illness, emotional illness, or social illness, or as projection of the problem to one or more children.

Elaine Harwood lived at a distance from her family so that she need not deal directly with her father. In fact, Elaine was more emotionally attached to her father than she was ready to admit. It is quite likely that the relationship between Elaine and her husband was characterized by emotional distance. This, compounded by the husband's alcoholism, worked to undermine the marriage.

The Family Projection Process

The family projection process is similar to the triangling process, except that it operates *specifically between parents and children.* Parents focus their anxiety on their children rather than dealing with the anxiety in their own relationship. The problem is not the person or the issue. It is the degree of anxiety and the emotionally reactive ways of dealing with it.

Anxiety is the *response* to stress, not stress itself. It is the anxiety reaction to stress that produces problems and symptoms. People can be terribly stressed and not too anxious. People in relationship systems are different when they are anxious than when they are calm. Anxiety can inundate the brain and keep it from working efficiently, biasing one's observations of self and others. It is infectious. As a person picks up another person's anxiety, he quickly responds and feeds anxiety back through the system, so that it inundates all the members.

Charles Harwood's case provides an example of the projection process. Louis, Sr. experienced great anxiety and distress over the death of his brother. He projected this anxiety onto his son Charles. This was much to the disadvantage of Charles, who proceeded to internalize the anxiety and abuse alcohol and drugs as he attempted to cope with the forces and pressures in his life.

Parents diffuse anxiety by focusing on a child. In this way they project part of their immaturity on the child. That child, in turn, becomes increasingly attached to the parent or parents doing the projecting and grows up less differentiated.

Examples of children who are likely to be objects of parents' projection are:

1. The child who is emotionally special to the mother or who is perceived by the mother to be emotionally special to the father.
2. The only girl among brothers or the only boy among sisters.
3. The child who follows the death of a child.
4. The first child.
5. The only child.
6. The child who was conceived or born during a period of stress for the mother.
7. The child with a handicap.
8. Twins.

Over generations members of a family emerge with higher, equal, or lower levels of differentiation. People tend to marry and establish intimate relationships with people who have similar levels of differentiation. When a person with a low level of differentiation marries a person with a low level of differentiation, they generally raise children with even lower levels of differentiation. Over time and generations, that family produces children with lower and lower levels of differentiation, until severe emotional problems result. The multigenerational process can be stopped and reversed, but only when people recognize their levels of differentiation and work to raise them.

The Importance of Sibling Position

The effect of birth position on personality and behavior is a frequently debated topic in family systems theory. Walter Toman, a clinical psychologist, did extensive research on birth order or rank, the sex mix of siblings, and the equivalent data about a person's same-sex, role-model parent. From his findings, Toman suggested patterns of behavior that people develop in families.

Toman began with the premise that the family is the most influential context in a person's life, that it exerts its influence in a regular, exclusive way early on. He confirmed Bowen's view that a person's position in the family structure strongly influences the expectations that person brings to situations throughout life.[2]

In particular, Toman examined the roles of the oldest child, the youngest child, the middle child, and the only child in the family structure. He also observed that the spacing of births influences how birth order or rank is applied. When there is an age difference of *six or more years* between successive siblings, the two tend to influence each other less than siblings who are closer in age. When six or more years separate siblings, there is effectively a new family structure, with the younger sibling becoming another oldest child.

1. *The oldest child.* In *The Matriarch,* G. B. Stern writes: "I'm the oldest of the oldest of the oldest. . . . And so I shall always do just as I like, and knock down everybody, and everybody will love me best, because I'm the oldest of the oldest of the oldest."[3]

So it is with the first-born child. This child arrives on the scene as very special. His parents have been waiting to be parents. They have experienced nothing like it before, so the child receives a great deal of attention. Because he is first, the child is expected to take on responsibilities for younger siblings; thus, he is pushed into a leadership role and is expected to be in charge. Oldest children tend to care for, guide, and protect the siblings that follow. Because of their age supremacy, they expect to be in charge and control.

2. *The youngest child.* Like the first-born child, the youngest child is special because he marks the end of a process. Youngest children expect to be in the company of other people because from the beginning they were never alone. Youngest children seek to be understood by others. This inward focus is in marked contrast to the outward focus of the older child, who seeks to understand the world about him. Sometimes youngest children are carefree, even to the point of irresponsibility, because an older sibling took responsibility for them. Younger children tend to consult with an older person. Typically, they are competitive but willing to acquiesce since they always had siblings who were older, more knowledgeable, and physically more powerful.

3. *The middle child.* There is not much special about middle children. They are not first or last. Even though they were the youngest at one point, it was only a temporary position. As a result, middle children have difficulty getting recognition. Eleanor Estes said it very well in *The Middle Moffat:*

When Mama introduced Sylvie, she always said, "This is Sylvie, my oldest child."
When Mama introduced Rufus, she always said, "This is Rufus, the baby in the family."
When Mama introduced Joey to people, she would say "This is Joey, my oldest son."
When Mama introduced Jane, she just said, "This is Jane." Because Mama had not figured out that Jane was the middle Moffat. Nobody had figured this out, but Jane.[4]

Since they tend not to get special recognition within the family, middle children either look outside the family structure for recognition or exert extraordinary pressure for recognition within the family. The middle child combines some of the roles of the older and the younger. Relative to his older siblings, he is younger and thus has some of the qualities of the younger child, such as taking direction. With respect to his younger siblings, he is older and thus has some of the qualities of the older child, such as taking the lead. Many middle children become very effective negotiators as adults simply because they had to negotiate for the resources in their sibling structure. Some psychologists say middle children tend to be better adjusted than those in other birth positions.

4. *The only child.* Only children have a sense of their specialness because they carry all the hopes, dreams, and aspirations of their parents. From the beginning, they must interact with adults, so it is not surprising that only children often seek the attention of authority figures. When only children enter their first structured learning situation, they may well stand aside and watch in amazement as their peers play with one another. After an adjustment period, they join in with the others and gradually learn effective interactive behaviors. They simply are not as well prepared for contact with peers as children who grew up with siblings. Only children learn to play by themselves and thus may be seen as somewhat aloof.

They view the world as quite complete without other people. They don't need them.

The Sex Mix of Siblings

Toman also concluded that the sex mix of siblings can have a great impact on future family, and nonfamily, relationships. People growing up in a family with children of both sexes learn to intimately interact and live with members of the opposite sex. People who grow up in a single-sex sibling structure have not shared a life at home with a peer of the opposite sex and are generally not as skilled at relating to the opposite sex.

In his analysis of over 3,000 marriages, Toman defined three types of relationships: complementary, noncomplementary, and doubly noncomplementary.

1. *The complementary relationship.* In a complementary relationship there is no conflict over rank and each partner had an opposite-sex sibling. Thus, if one partner in a marriage is an oldest child and had younger siblings of the opposite sex and one partner is the youngest child and had older siblings of the opposite sex, little conflict will predictably occur between them in terms of control and natural interaction. In their family structure, they have learned to deal effectively with the opposite sex. In Toman's sample, there were no divorces among couples having complementary relationships.

2. *The noncomplementary relationship.* In a noncomplementary relationship there is conflict over either rank *or* sex. If the conflict is over rank, there will be problems of control. For example, when two oldest children marry, they will both want to be in charge. If the conflict is over sex, the partners have trouble relating to the opposite sex because neither had an opposite-sex sibling. Conflict over sex does not refer to disagreement regarding sexual intimacy but rather to difficulties in sharing day-to-day life with a member of the opposite sex.

For example, girls from an all-female sibling structure often learn too late about boys' leaving the toilet seat up; boys without sisters don't learn about the subtleties of menstruation.

3. *The doubly noncomplementary relationship.* In a doubly noncomplementary relationship there is conflict over *both* rank and sex. An example is a marriage between an oldest brother of brothers and an oldest sister of sisters. These partners would probably always vie for control, since they are both the oldest and accustomed to being in charge. Since neither had a sibling of the opposite sex in the family, they would be at a further disadvantage in sharing a life.

In Toman's study, the divorce rate in doubly noncomplementary relationships was twice that of the entire sample. These partners brought into the marriage systems messages that ultimately undermined it. Each wanted and, in fact, expected control and couldn't learn to share it. In addition, neither was really prepared to deal with intimate day-to-day life with the other.

Other Factors

Other factors modify Toman's basic theory. One factor is the same data about one's same-sex parent. A boy watches his father and from him learns how a man is expected to act. A girl watches her mother, who serves as a model for how a woman is expected to act. Therefore, the birth position is tempered or reinforced by some of the qualities the parents provided as role models for their children. A person who is an oldest and whose same-sex parent is a youngest will have behaviors characteristic of oldest and of youngest. The degree of dominance will depend on the number of other siblings. This is where one must exercise careful judgment and discretion in applying the theory.

The death or illness of a sibling, the work patterns of parents, adoptions, the death of a parent, divorce, and the intermixing of children from previous marriages can also influence personality development. The age at which these events occur and one's place in the family determine the extent of the influence.

One must be cautious, of course, about applying any theory of human behavior. Evidence suggests that the very reverse can occur in cases of extreme opposites.[5] It would take a separate book to compare and debate the widely diverse conclusions; however, the research of Swiss psychiatrists Cecile Ernst and Jules Angst, who refute many of Toman's conclusions, should be mentioned.[6] In my view Ernst and Angst failed to include in their analysis many of the available studies that Toman cited. In addition, Ernst and Angst did not adequately correlate with Toman's work the studies that they claimed disproved birth order theory.

In conclusion, all the studies and research in the world will not change the fact that, in some families, position of birth and sex mix of siblings *can* affect the personality development of children. It has much to do with how those positions are perceived by the parents, and the correlating expectations and responsibilities assigned to them.

Conflict and Change

Many people have the mistaken idea that the measure of the successful or the healthy family is the lack of conflict. On the contrary, it is *a family's ability to manage and resolve conflict that determines its maturity and emotional health.* That, of course, is also the true measure of an individual's maturity and emotional health. In fact, conflict is often a catalyst for change, which in turn is a healthy, normal, even necessary function of living.

Leaving the family, breaking away in any mode, does not always translate into resolving the conflicts that are part of the fabric of family ties. Neither is it the same as "growing up." Perhaps the greatest tragedy in thinking that family conflicts are escaped by leaving them is that they carry over unresolved, into the next generation. The very same conflicts and problems that caused people the most pain as children, and continue to cause them great pain as adults, are passed on to their own children.

In the presence of severe family problems, efforts ordinarily spent in planning ahead are diverted into maintaining the status quo, however stressful. Families then resist change, because they are preoccupied with balancing the present, which often takes the form of attempting to remove symptoms in one person or one relationship. For example, Elaine Harwood must tackle the unresolved issues with her father in order to become more well differentiated. If she does not, then it is likely that she will transmit her lower level of differentiation to her children.

Change in families is difficult because it demands that people not only look at but also adjust beliefs that have been developed over a lifetime and that often come from previous generations. But for change to occur, inherited beliefs and values must be questioned. Values are the core of the family structure. To examine values, then, families must be examined, for values are the property of family systems first and of individual members afterward.

There are benefits in looking at family systems. For example, the individual discovers:

1. Discrete patterns of behavior that help or hinder relationships.
2. Family messages that explain attitudes, feelings, and actions.

3. The way the family handles communications and resolves or denies conflicts.
4. Alternatives for solving problems more efficiently and effectively.

Family behavior patterns stem from family rules. The greatest dysfunction is caused by rules that are rigid or hidden. The goal of family systems therapy is to bring hidden rules to the surface and to loosen rigid rules so that patterns that create pain and keep family members from establishing themselves as individuals can be eliminated. Families can then be flexible as they move from one stage to another. The goal of applying family systems theory in business is to identify family patterns that impair operations or impede progress. Once the impact of those patterns is minimized, the family enterprise can grow, prosper, and maximize profit. The family willing to do this will derive the greatest possible level of satisfaction from the family business.

4

Interpreting the Family System

A family is first and foremost a unit of people whose relationships and functioning are interconnected. The family is a system that transmits messages. Members interact on the basis of the messages sent. The family system can create, learn, and adapt to other patterns of behavior, but the family *will* revert to original patterns unless it learns to modify behavior.

With this in mind, let's return to our study of the Harwood family. The Harwoods—like all families with business difficulties—faced four key tasks:

1. To identify and understand the behavioral messages being passed within the family, especially patterns that might be in opposition to sound business practice.
2. To understand how these family messages affect the business operation.
3. To make the necessary modifications in the way the family functions so the negative behavior of the family has a minimum impact on the business enterprise.

4. To move the business to a more professional level of operation by using the skills and talents of family and nonfamily members.

The Family Genogram

The fabric woven by a family in business is as rich as that of any Shakespearean play. Initially, characteristics are viewed as germane to the individual, but as the players interact and the threads of the play intertwine, the qualities of one character influence the others. Sometimes the audience can correctly predict what will happen. Many times there are surprises.

To help unravel the family plot, it is useful to draw a genogram, or family systems map. The purpose of the genogram is to enable family members to develop sufficient objectivity about themselves and their entire "cast" to accurately identify the strengths and vulnerabilities of each player. Then all of them will be better able to predict the outcomes and *even write their own ending* to the family business play.

The symbols and guidelines shown in Figure 3 are useful in constructing a family genogram. Most of these symbols come into play in the Harwood family genogram shown in Figure 4.

The Family Message Chart

The next step is to examine the critical family relationships in the genogram and to construct a "message chart." As all the messages sent through members of the family are written down, invariably, common messages emerge. (Keep in mind that there are always exceptions—things that "fall off the wall" and must be interpreted.) Look first at the birth position of each individual, then at the sex mix of the siblings. Look at the same data for the same-sex parent.

Look at the goals in the family. What were the members expected to do? Were they expected to be well educated? Were they expected to develop social skills? Were they expected to be involved in the community? Note all the things that have to do with family function.

Next, look at the decision making in the family and the control of decisions, especially financial control. This will usually say something about what a family does with its resources. Then look at how the family manages conflict. Is it open debate or do the parents argue in the bedroom with the door closed? Or is nothing said? Look at how the father and mother handle conflict between themselves and then how it is handled in the family.

Look at the communications patterns in terms of the completeness of communication and in terms of sharing information. This will give you an inkling about secrets in the family.

Figure 5 shows the messages being sent by Louis, Sr. and Lillian Harwood to their children.

Sometimes it is useful to set a genogram aside and let it "percolate." Over time, messages will become more clear and well understood and can be added to a master genogram that contains all the information gathered. For example, at first Elaine's situation might not be apparent. However, after another look it should become clear that her position as first-born suggests a need to take control. This need is tempered by her mother's position and style, specifically to have opinions but to take a lower profile and defer to her husband or older brother. Louis, Jr.'s acceptance of his role in the company can be explained in part by his younger position, and his ability to get things done can be seen to stem from the model of both parents, in which contributing, controlling, and taking charge play a major part.

47

Figure 3. Instructions on preparing symbols for a family genogram.

1. Use squares for men ☐ , and circles for women ○ . Add ages when appropriate.

2. Place the husband on the left and draw a solid line to the wife on the right.

☐────────────○

3. Indicate marriage by the symbol "m." and the date.

☐──────m. 1950──────○

4. Indicate birth order of children from left to right. Include, if known:
   a. full names and nicknames.
   b. birth and death dates, plus locations.
   c. dates and places of marriages.

5. If a person is deceased, put a cross through the symbol.

⊠   ⊗

6. If a child is adopted, put a dotted line to the marriage line connecting the child to the adoptive parents. Indicate age of adoption.

☐ or ○

7. For a miscarriage or a stillbirth, use a solid triangle if the sex is unknown. Use a dotted circle or square if the sex is known. Connect to the parents with a solid line.

8. For an abortion, use a triangle with a circle in it. Connect to the parents with a solid line.

48

9. For a separation, put a single line through the marriage line and date it.

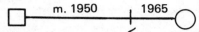

10. For a divorce, use the symbol 〉 d. through the marriage line. Show the date and the parent with custody of the children.

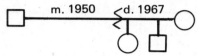

11. For a second marriage or subsequent marriages, indicate the number of the marriage with the date.

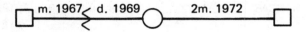

12. For multiple births, draw a solid line and place a box(es) or a circle(s) at the end as appropriate.

13. For ease of reference indicate the number of years between siblings.

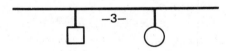

The Win-Lose Factor

The final step in untangling the relationships within a family is to examine how the family handles "winning" and "losing." What happens, for example, when people in a family make a mistake? Everybody makes mistakes sometimes. In some fami-

Figure 4. The Harwood family genogram.

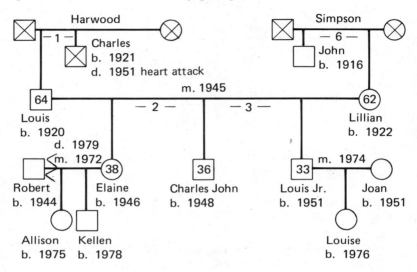

lies the mistake is brushed off and everyone says: "Well, what can we learn from it?" In other families everyone says: "Hey, dummy. You did it again." A positive orientation—namely, a win-win approach—is essential to establishing a productive work environment within the family business. Only then can all parties within the family business feel good about their work and their contributions.

Simply stated, *if there are two parties to a transaction, there are three potential outcomes: win-win, win-lose, and lose-lose.*

1. *Win-win.* In a win-win situation, both parties *feel* positive about the outcome. Each party shares in the beneficial results of the transaction. Notice the emphasis on the word *feel.* If people feel that they shared in the beneficial outcomes, then it is pointless to split hairs over the exact distribution of rewards.

An excellent way to demonstrate win-win is for two people to stand facing one another with palms touching. Each

Figure 5. The Harwood family message chart.

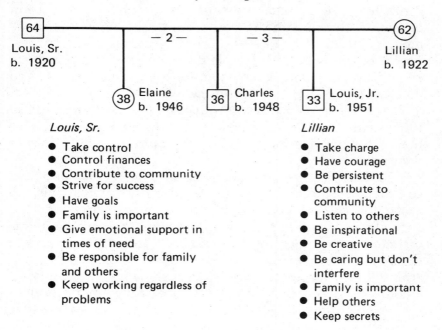

Louis, Sr.

- Take control
- Control finances
- Contribute to community
- Strive for success
- Have goals
- Family is important
- Give emotional support in times of need
- Be responsible for family and others
- Keep working regardless of problems

Lillian

- Take charge
- Have courage
- Be persistent
- Contribute to community
- Listen to others
- Be inspirational
- Be creative
- Be caring but don't interfere
- Family is important
- Help others
- Keep secrets

Combined Family Messages of Louis, Sr. and Lillian Harwood

- Be in charge, take control
- Contribute to community
- Create; have goals
- Never give up
- Problems should never interfere
- Family is important
- Be responsible
- Be devoted to what you are doing
- Secrets between family members are acceptable

223651

maintains enough pressure to cause the other's hands to move gently left or right. Equal pressure will cause the hands to be in balance, with neither party overpowering the other. The hands move gently in sync in a vertical plane between the parties. This it is win-win. Both people maintain enough pressure to keep the other person's hands in the air, but neither exerts so much pressure as to overpower the other.

2. *Win-lose.* In a win-lose situation, one party receives *all* the benefits from the transaction while the other party receives none. One party feels good about the outcome, and the other does not.

To demonstrate a win-lose situation, one person applies a considerable amount of pressure to the other's hands. This will cause the second person's hands to move backward. The natural response is to push back. It encourages pushing in one direction or the other, forward and back. In fact, this increases the physical tension between the two people. Each is likely to attempt to overpower the other. Ultimately, a significant amount of energy is expended until one or the other prevails.

3. *Lose-lose.* In a lose-lose situation, both parties feel they received none of the beneficial outcomes of the transaction.

To demonstrate a lose-lose situation, one party withdraws from contact—the hands do not touch. Now it is impossible for either party to influence the other, because there is no vehicle for communication.

The least amount of combined energy is expended in the win-win transaction, where each party maintains a sufficient amount of pressure but does not attempt to overpower the other. In a healthy business, there is a maximum amount of win-win behavior with a minimum amount of inappropriate win-lose. Notice the use of the word "inappropriate." Sometimes it is proper to have a win-lose situation—one party is right while another party is wrong.

When a family member says, "I'm right, and you are wrong," it is a win-lose. If the family member to whom this is said withdraws and knuckles under, it is a lose-lose. On the other hand, the person who says, "Let's discuss the options available and see which one seems to fit this circumstance," is inviting a win-win approach from the other family member.

Choosing a win-win strategy upon entering a transaction makes it possible for the outcome to be win-win. IF at the outset a win-lose strategy is elected, there are only two possible outcomes: win-lose or lose-lose. The transaction will *not* escalate upward to win-win, and the participants are restricted to the two lesser outcomes.

The win-win theory couples directly with research on the motivation of personnel. Employees want to feel good (positive) about their work and about their work environment. Further, they want to feel that they can influence their own circumstances and make a contribution to their job. The win-win environment permits all of this.

Once a family's genogram is constructed, its messages interpreted, and the win-lose factor evaluated, Act I of the family play is finished. What will clearly result is a better understanding of the relationships among family members and the way they interact.

Act II of the family play addresses other factors that complicate the relationships among family members. Some of these factors are directly responsible for the way relationships are played out, for the choices that are made in the family business, and for the outcome of the family play itself. Let's begin by looking more closely at some of the major players in the drama.

5

The Entrepreneur

A major problem confronting a family enterprise is that of succession. An enormous amount of time and energy is devoted to planning for a smooth transition from the founder to the next generation of management. But even the most carefully constructed plans will be academic unless four major underlying factors are understood:

1. The entrepreneurial personality (traditionally male) and its relation to power and control.
2. The role of the family women.
3. Substance abuse.
4. Sound business practice.

These issues often lie at the core of the family's business problems, either singly or in combination.

Considerable material has been written about the entrepreneurial personality. None of it, including what is said here, can be classified as hard-and-fast research data. It is basically opinion, observation, and experience. However, from this material specific traits and facts emerge so frequently that a profile can be created. Not all entrepreneurs have each and every trait in the profile, but many manifest a preponderance of them.

Before examining these traits, it is relevant to note that most of the source material written before 1980 has been about men, who appeared to be dominant among entrepreneurs. This may be a cultural bias on the part of business researchers and historians that statistical data will not support. Nonetheless, the term "entrepreneur" presently has a male-gender connotation: Generally women who achieve success in a "man's field" have not been considered entrepreneurial but simply exceptional women.

For the most part, behaviors that characterize the entrepreneur have been discouraged in the generation of women now between 40 and 65. It is prudent to predict that when the generation now 25 to 38 reaches 40-plus, we will see a great many women entrepreneurs. The term will eventually lose its gender connotation. Again, though male-gender words are used for convenience in this discussion, "he" should be understood to refer to both sexes unless otherwise specified.

Daddy or Demagogue?

Every first-generation family business was started by a person with a vision of a successful product or service. Entrepreneurship is the essence of the American business spirit. Inside the family circle, reactions to the entrepreneur are principally emotional. This creates a whole set of issues that spill over into daily business decisions. Either success is achieved at an extravagant personal price or failure dominates the scenario because others fail to help at crucial moments.

The traditional profile of the entrepreneur presents two

extremes. One is a benevolent dictator who shapes an idea into reality, then relinquishes control. The other is of a controlling devastator who gives, then takes away, and in the end threatens to destroy everything he has built by his need for absolute control. Most entrepreneurs fall somewhere within this continuum.

Interaction with the entrepreneur also runs to extremes. Almost everyone has a favorite story about him that ends with the words, "What a character!" In part the behavior of an entrepreneur stems from his need to birth his vision *as he sees it*. In part it is also a reaction to those around him who perceive only the intense drive in his personality.

Anyone starting a company needs to understand this inner motivation, as do those who work with the entrepreneur. Without a thorough understanding of what can be expected, lawyers, accountants, and other business professionals cannot help solve an entrepreneur's problems.

Another noticeable characteristic of the entrepreneur is the urge and ability to take risks and maintain faith in his daring decisions. Strongly independent, he has a highly developed creativity, a desire for recognition, and a peculiar sense of time and timing. He identifies totally with his enterprise. Also, he is likely to be the first-born or eldest surviving child.

From the beginning of life, a first-born child has a feeling of being in charge and wants to control matters. Parents place special expectations on him. He is expected, for example, to care for younger siblings, because he is the "oldest." He resists functioning under strong authority figures. In fact, he resents anyone telling him what to do. Later, in his business life, the independent attitude translates into the need for total domination of the enterprise. He feels *compelled* to control everything. This has negative consequences for sound business practice.

Typically, the entrepreneur wants to know everything going on throughout his empire, but he does not want to be bothered with the minutiae connected with management. The details that are so essential to a finely tuned, well-managed business are likely to bore him. He can compensate for this by hiring skilled managers to attend to the ever present details. If he does not, numerous problems arise, not the least of which is failure. This entrepreneur's dream and determination can carry him only so far.

Case histories suggest that a significant number of entrepreneurs have experienced massive psychic upheavals during key developmental stages. These include the death of a meaningful person, family disruptions, estrangement from one or both parents, and poverty. Such problems complicate movement in normal developmental stages, especially during the teenage years, when the child begins to separate from the parents. As his unique personality emerges, the child begins to shift responsibility away from the parents and take it on himself. This includes resolving authority figure issues, usually with the father.

A child whose parent is absent or unavailable during adolescence does not have the opportunity to develop the skills that are essential in dealing with authority figures later on in life. The search for emotional expression is further undermined by the need to assume responsibility without a proper role model to turn to for advice. Skills for effectively communicating emotions are pushed into the background as the need to "get on" with life preempts the expression of feelings.

The Lifetime Learner

The typical business leader graduates from high school and goes on to college. This is not necessarily the case with entrepreneurs. It is not unusual for them to interrupt formal education to become self-taught, lifetime learners. Today's new crop is no exception. In April 1985, *Rolling Stone* magazine reported that of 40 millionaire entrepreneurs under age 30 only two had college degrees. And these two were making less money than the others. Apparently, the entrepreneurial drive overcomes the usual educational goals regardless of the social climate or family tradition.

Typically, the North American male has between three to seven distinct career explorations between ages 20 and 30. Although these false or half starts are normal, the would-be entrepreneur encounters a specific difficulty. Someone else is always the boss. His unresolved authority issues surface as he learns a lot about the world of work but finds it difficult to accept another person directing his life. He feels the need to create a work situation for himself.

The majority of entrepreneurs begin their first business at age 30 to 35. In times of social upheaval, such as war or technological change, the age lowers. This has happened recently in the computer and communications industries.

Sometimes an emerging entrepreneur will be older. Lulled into security by a job with a high salary, stock options, bonuses, and profit sharing, he does not make a leap into business until his forties. Often more radical than his younger counterpart, he changes not only his business direction but his personal lifestyle.

Women generally start their entrepreneurships later than men. One reason is that they believe they need the maximum formal education to compete with men in business. It is not uncommon for the woman entrepreneur to have a Master's degree or other advanced certification. Another factor is family responsibility. Women normally wait to begin a business venture until their children are out of school and time and money become more available. Also, the woman entrepreneur of the 1980s may be a single parent. She may start a business at home as a needed first or second income while eliminating child care problems.

The Entrepreneur's Vision

Another trait shared by entrepreneurial personalities is the ability to envision unusual connections and possibilities. Many products and services have come into being because an entrepreneur can see how to revolutionize a product, turn around an industry, or change consumer habits. His creativity allows him to design the plan in which all the pieces lead to success. Imagination, a subsidiary function to creativity, is used mainly for problem solving.

The vision of the entrepreneur is a powerful force for making dreams become reality. He is consumed by "the idea." His intensity gives him charisma: He is exciting to work for and fascinating to be around. However, he can be a real "rascal" in the opportunistic sense, as he takes liberties with established ways of doing things. He will readily sacrifice his security, and that of his family, to advance "the idea." He loves the excitement and challenge of risk. In fact, he will often pass over opportunities that do not offer it. In the hurried race to implement "the idea," he may fail to communicate clearly with the people he needs to help him realize success. This can include everyone from his banker to his spouse to his children. Consequently, he comes to believe he must do everything if it is to be done "right."

Sometimes the entrepreneur has no clear sense of his personality. As he becomes more closely identified with the business, anything that happens to *it* is interpreted as happening to *him* personally. He rejects anyone who questions him and becomes defensive. This presents a number of problems in a family business.

A family member who wants to change a procedure is confronted by a dictatorial entrepreneur. Orderly change is defeated. The tunnel vision that made the entrepreneur's idea a reality turns against him and stands in the way of professionalizing his business operation. A business needs entrepreneurship to get on its feet, but it must grow into a professionally managed operation to survive. This is a critical point many entrepreneurs overlook or reject.

Another trait of most entrepreneurs is a peculiar sense of time. This has led many who work with them to conclude that entrepreneurs believe they will never die. In fact, some entrepreneurs will state that emphatically. A deeper look gives another answer.

Rarely does the entrepreneur fear dying or entertain thoughts of dying. He is too busy making his ideas come to pass. He lives in an ever constant present or in a mental future where time is not governed by sunrises and sunsets. Rather, time is governed by cycles of productivity, goals achieved, and profits reached.

When making a decision for the future, the entrepreneur does not include death in his calculations. As the ultimate risk-taker, he downgrades death to an insignificant factor. He reasons that his business, product, or service will live after him. He will never die unless the business does. This attitude complicates succession. When letting go of the business is the entrepreneur's equivalent of death, he must be convinced that the business will stay in capable hands. "But who knows as much as I do?" he asks. Consequently, he must decide for himself if other goals are still to be reached, so he can let go of his "old" self/business and move onward.

Though the entrepreneur wants recognition for his achievements, he is usually not concerned solely with power. Power is important to him only insofar as it brings his vision into material being. However, money is important to him—it is a way to measure his success—and he enjoys accumulating it. Let's look at a few examples.

The Entrepreneur Patriarch: Louis Harwood, Sr.

Louis Harwood, Sr. fulfilled all the characteristics of the entrepreneur. As the eldest son, he accepted responsibility for his family when his father died while Louis was in his teens.

He believed fervently in the product designed by his brother, Charles, and saw its potential to the growing aircraft industry. After he alone raised the capital to begin the company, he worked hard to ensure that the product would become known and valued. He boldly pursued the military contracts that vaulted Harwood E&C to a high level of prosperity. His risks paid off: The company grew into a solid enterprise.

For Louis, the early years of the company were a thrilling time. As corporate parent, he knew all phases of the business intimately. Never did he lose touch with the manufacturing, marketing, or administrative ends. In addition, he enjoyed it. After Charles's death, he redefined goals for himself and the company. His decisions were always identified with the growth of the business, and his personality became intertwined with its success.

Louis's brother had maintained a peripheral, "helping" role in the business. Louis perceived his sons in the same way. Son Charles became a confidant and friend who listened to business problems. Son Louis could not become a full-fledged member of the business because his personality did not fit his father's image of an entrepreneur. Louis, Sr. did not realize that the business had become an extension of himself. If he had not encountered health problems, he probably would not have thought about the future of the business. He had never made plans for a successor—a common plight among entrepreneurs.

Louis Harwood demonstrates only one type of entrepreneurial thinking. It is worthwhile to look at others to put his profile into perspective. Again, these examples are composites, not actual people.

The Enfant Terrible: Charlie Lake

At age sixty, Charlie Lake was not about to slow down. Charlie inherited a budding manufacturing business, broadened its potential, and took it to a new plane of success. A

veteran pilot of World War II, Charlie attacked success, prepared to shoot down everything that stood in the way of his
mission.

Charlie's problem was that of succession. Melinda, his
only heir, had no wish to follow her father in business. Her
husband, Andrew, did work in the family business. When
Charlie did not credit Andrew with the talent and skills he
obviously possessed, Andrew left the company to develop his
own enterprise. The two remained outwardly cordial to each
other, but their relationship grew tense. They said less and less
to each other and made no effort to correct the problem. Two
years later, the problem solved itself in a very roundabout way.

After more than twenty-five years of marriage, Charlie
divorced his first wife. With his second marriage, Charlie's
interest in the day-to-day operation of the business diminished
as he traveled the world with his new bride. This led to his
decision to step down from daily operations and give his son-
in-law the opportunity to run the company.

Without asking Andrew if he wanted the opportunity,
Charlie *announced* his decision to his successor. Andrew, taken
aback by the sudden, apparent reversal in his father-in-law's
attitude, asked for time to consider the proposal. Charlie
perceived this as a refusal and a lack of appreciation for the
opportunity. He felt rejected and hurt. The move triggered an
examination of the real problems involved.

Charlie had never had to deal with the succession problem
because his father had simply handed the business over to
him. He grew up with the knowledge that he would go into his
father's business, which he did in the late 1940s, when it was a
fledgling operation. By the mid-1960s, the gross sales were in
the single-digit millions. Twenty years later, the gross *profits*
were running that much. Charlie Lake was recognized by his
peers as a marketing genius.

Charlie was the classic entrepreneur consumed by his
business. He had a bombastic style—demanding, compulsive,

and filled with expectation. He dominated the company. Every decision had to pass his desk, whether it involved the advertising program, sales efforts and promotions, or manufacturing. He communicated a constant sense of urgency and was quick to take the initiative in problem solving. A chain of command could be broken on the spur of the moment if Charlie stepped into the middle of a problem and made a decision. Employees were often embarrassed by public scoldings for what Charlie identified as incorrect decisions or unworkable ideas.

Charlie's personal life reflected the same need to take risks and stay in command. He loved flying and piloted his own corporate jet. He favored golf and other nonteam sports.

Charlie did have a generous side, which extended to his daughter, Melinda, and her husband. Trips to foreign countries, stock, money gifts, loans—all were readily extended but not forgotten. Although he would never admit it, Charlie wanted to be recognized for his generosity. He was hurt if the response he got was not the one he *believed* he deserved.

In summary, he was a dynamic, intelligent man who pursued what he wanted and was not satisfied until he got it. His vision paid off in peer recognition and a large personal fortune, which he was not reluctant to spend. He carefully protected his business, the "golden goose" of his lifestyle, from any outside disruption. In the eyes of others, he was a formidable man. Charlie Lake enjoyed it that way.

Charlie's profile raises key questions that many family businesses face. Is it possible to work with an entrepreneur who always gets what he wants even if he has to change the ground rules to do so? Can the family messages be changed from win-lose to win-win relationships for everyone? Can behaviors be established that allow Charlie and his second wife to relate to Melinda and Andrew, both professionally and personally, in a manner that will add positive strokes to their respective lives? Finally, is it possible for the son-in-law to learn to trust Charlie and return to the business? Can Charlie allow his successor, especially another entrepreneurial type, to take control?

In the end, as we will see, Charlie Lake moved to find solutions to his family's business problems because he loved his child and his enterprise. His entrepreneurial courage did not fail him in his greatest risk venture: family life. Further, once the plan was developed, he and Andrew worked amicably together to implement each detail.

The Rollover Entrepreneur: Blake Williams

Blake Williams developed and expressed his entrepreneurial skills in marked contrast to Charlie Lake. As the oldest child in a large family, he was always expected to do well. Because he matured in the years of World War II, his military service came before his career. After the war, he attended college and majored in business. He started a self-service laundry business with a partner while he was still in school.

The pattern of hard work and selfless devotion to an idea, which is common to entrepreneurs, surfaced in the pace the young man set for himself. In addition to a full school workload, he devoted around-the-clock attention to his laundry business. Within a year, he expanded the operation, offering his services as a consultant to those wishing to set up similar service centers. Finally, he and his partner sold the business and Blake went to work for an organization headed by an uncle.

Blake stayed with that business for almost ten years. His increasing knowledge led to new solutions to problems that plagued the industry. Eventually he left the business to become a broker for sales services in the same field. Then, an established company came on the market. Blake bought it, installed state-of-the-art equipment, and began to implement some of his service ideas. In succeeding years, he bought more companies, extending the capacity of his operation and the quality of service he had envisioned as possible. He soon had a virtual empire of services that raised the quality expectation of customers in the industry.

His associates saw him as an aggressive, hard-working, competitive, and visionary leader whose monetary success was merely a way of keeping score in the game of life. What really mattered to him, they believed, was the enjoyment he got from putting businesses on sound financial footing. They were correct.

Blake's business philosophy was to bring an enterprise to a certain stage of growth and turn it loose to achieve its potential. He did the same with his children. Each child had been invited to come into the business, but three chose other careers. Blake accepted this, though he stipulated that they learn enough about the family business to protect their interests and responsibly manage the substantial sums that would accrue to them.

The greatest lesson in Blake's profile is that his entrepreneurial mind was channeled in a way that allowed him to plan for succession. His confidence to do this came from his success in "letting go" of his businesses. One of Blake's particular traits, uncommon among entrepreneurs, was the ability to allow a business he had rescued from financial disaster to fly on its own. He refinanced, restructured, and reorganized management and procedures, then tested the business's ability to stand alone. Blake employed these same principles in planning for his own retirement from business. His genius was in knowing when the time was right for success and succession to occur. All family businesses can gain confidence from his example. Family and business need not be considered oil and water.

As these examples show, when looking for the root of the problems encountered in family business, it is essential to look first to the entrepreneur. If his traits, positive and negative, are not dealt with openly and intelligently, only disaster can result. Families can tear themselves apart over the very person who made their business great. By recognizing what composes the entrepreneur's personality, other family members begin to understand him. They can then begin to build a unity within their business. Real problems that were unappreciated as contributing to the difficulties at hand are solved when the family realizes entrepreneurs *are* different from other people.

Entrepreneurship has been maligned for the very reason that it succeeds—dedication. The entrepreneur must understand himself as well as be understood by others. The vision that brought the company into being is different from the skills that will keep it going over generations. There comes a time when the entrepreneur must distance himself from his company so that it can move forward. His business must have a successor generation so that it can move more into history than one unique personality. It can pass onto other generations a philosophy that binds a family together as it creates the rich traditions that make American society strong.

6

Wives and Daughters

In the American business tradition, taking a woman into the company was on a par with taking a woman to sea: bad luck at worst and a lot of trouble at best. A daughter was considered successful and useful if she married well. A wife was expected to be an extension of her husband's property. In fact, the idea of the woman as weak and incompetent persisted well into the twentieth century. Now, social and economic circumstances have jolted many women out of these limited roles and put them in charge of their lives.

Old attitudes are falling aside in the 1980s. Today, women are entering traditionally male-dominated fields in record numbers. They operate foundries, construction firms, and real estate companies. Women hold top positions in banking and finance. The United Mine Workers encourages women to run for district and international offices. In 1984, the Campbell Soup Company increased its number of women vice presidents from two to six. At Hallmark, 42 percent of the managers and professionals in the company's largest plant are women. According to the Small Business Administration's Office of Women's Business Ownership, 3 million women own businesses grossing more than $40 billion. The simple fact is, women *are* as suited to business and as successful in it as men.

The woman who tries to establish her identity in a family business faces quite different problems from her counterpart who leaves home to embark on a career. The latter has to prove her competency in a chosen field. Once she has done that, only her ambition and talent limit her success. The woman in a family business has to establish herself as a professional in the highly personal atmosphere of family. Elaine Harwood typifies this problem, and it is worthwhile to spin out in detail what happened to her.

The Entrepreneurial Daughter: Elaine Harwood

An intelligent young woman with excellent business skills, Elaine was overlooked because of her father's traditional attitude that women should not enter certain fields. Louis was happy with his wife's role in his business. Lillian listened to and supported his decisions. It never occurred to him that his daughter would want to assume a role other than the one her mother exemplified.

Elaine's family failed to recognize her entrepreneurial qualities. To her father, the drive toward a goal in the face of great odds was an exciting challenge and commitment. In Elaine, he labeled the same behavior as "being headstrong." The term confused Elaine and made her feel a little guilty about her drive, which took the edge off many of her achievements.

When Elaine decided on her college major—business and interior design—Louis envisioned her in a small shop somewhere nearby where she would advise local wives on their decorating problems. It was a pleasant "little project" from Louis's point of view, something to keep Elaine occupied until she found the right person to marry.

Elaine and her father never openly discussed her coming into Harwood Engine and Cable. She did a good job during her part-time employment there when she was in high school and college and received compliments from Louis. As she grew older, it was obvious that he would never seriously consider giving her a meaningful role in the company. Elaine considered her brother Charles merely a yes-man and was envious of his business pipeline to their father. But it was her father's treatment of the youngest child, Louis, Jr., that convinced her she could never be a part of the family enterprise. If her father was blind to Lou's interest and talents, what could *she* expect?

Still, the problem of succession had to be dealt with. The easiest way out: "Do nothing." In that case, if Louis, Sr. died and no successor was groomed, Lillian would probably have to sell the business for a price lower than its fair market value.

Another alternative was to choose and begin grooming a successor immediately. This was a hard task for Louis, Sr. to face. He did not want his life's work to come to nothing for lack of planning, but it was difficult for him to accept anyone at the helm, *including another family member.* In the end, his love for what he had built and his fervent desire to see it continue made him accept the fact that a successor was necessary. He concluded that person would be Charles.

As their consultant, I suggested at this point that the family establish criteria for leadership of the company. Together, we developed a profile of the prerequisite skills of a successor. This done, I asked which family member, if any, had all the skills listed. Louis, Sr. was stunned. *Elaine fit the profile the family had created.* In the years she was becoming successful in her own right, he had seen her only as his capable daughter from whom he expected success in her "woman's world." When the gender issue was set aside and Elaine's skills and abilities were brought into focus, what Louis, Sr. had seen as detriments became the very talents he intuitively knew made her his ideal successor.

71

Family Business, Risky Business

Elaine's portfolio of experience had prepared her to take over the Harwood family business. Her entrepreneurial needs had been met, and when she came to Harwood Engine and Cable, Elaine was sure of her abilities and clear about her personality. Her anxiety focused on whether or not her father would allow her to be the professional she knew she was *and* the daughter she wanted to be. Many talented daughters face this problem and fail to solve it. The subsequent leadership loss has contributed to the shortened life of many family businesses.

The "Corporate Wife": Melinda Oakton

In contrast to Elaine Harwood is Melinda Lake Oakton. Melinda was satisfied to be a "corporate wife." She had enjoyed the atmosphere of power and prestige that her father generated. She saw her mother's role as "decorating" the social space her father provided. She also realized how much her father needed someone inside the family to rely on. Melinda was determined to provide this support for her husband, Andrew. To do this, she became quite knowledgeable about the business. She expanded his social world, provided emotional support, and kept herself intellectually active. Melinda and Andrew Oakton became a classic corporate marriage that worked.

When Charlie Lake and Andrew Oakton parted ways, Melinda was clear about her commitments to both of them. She understood how to share space with her father and with Andrew. Charlie did not, and Melinda recognized the obstacle. Because her own needs were satisfied and her intentions clear, Melinda was a strong force in helping her father accept Andrew as a peer.

She was able to express her deep feelings for Charlie *and* the business in a way he would eventually accept. He knew what Melinda wanted and how well she perceived his business

72

needs. At the same time, the successor problem did not envelop Melinda. Charlie knew she did not want to head his company, but she did want to keep it in the family. This meant Charlie had to confront the problems with his son-in-law.

The Overlooked Daughter: Maria Johnson

Not all successor daughters are as articulate about their desires as Melinda or as entrepreneurial as Elaine. The most commonly overlooked daughter is one who works in a business that employs all family members who wish to enter, but then divides their roles strictly along gender lines. The men handle finances and management, and set policy; the women handle the support skills and the paperwork. As the family begins to look for a successor, this daughter is never considered—solely because of gender.

For example, the Johnson family operated a construction supply company. Ben Johnson and his two sons held titles of president and vice presidents, Ben's wife was the secretary-treasurer, and their daughter headed the incoming order department. In addition, several male in-laws populated the sales staff and one sister-in-law was head bookkeeper. The daughter, Maria, wanted a greater role in the company, but lacked the formal business education that her two brothers had received. Since all roles were filled, and a top management position seemed closed to her, she became frustrated as the years passed and manifested her problem by becoming difficult for other family members to work with. Whenever she became particularly impossible, her youngest brother, Phil, was asked to talk to her.

In the discussions between them, they confided their frustrations to each other. Maria felt she knew enough about what the clients wanted and needed to step into the sales force. Phil hated the financial aspects of the business and wanted a more nuts-and-bolts job in which his decisions did not crucially

73

affect the entire company. Neither one of them had articulated their desires to other family members, least of all their father. (Note the triangling that takes place in this transaction.)

These unmet needs were undermining the business. Soon an outside mediator was asked to resolve the family's business problems. Both Maria and Phil wanted positions within the company that would fulfill their goals. The obvious solution was to move the daughter to the sales force and the unhappy son to a less demanding spot. In professional management, the talents and ambitions of these two individuals would be taken into consideration regardless of gender or birth order. A family in business needs to remember it has to operate the business end of itself in a professional way if its profits are to grow and its tradition is to survive.

In a case like this, finding the potential successor is difficult. Each family member has excellent experience, but not all qualified members have the desire to run the enterprise. When the successor profile is drawn and a daughter who lacks specific important skills emerges as the most qualified, the family is unclear about what it should do. The solution is simply to train the daughter in the techniques she needs to run the business. A number of leadership and management training programs teach these skills. The next part of her training would be with a mentor, either within the business or outside of it, who would guide and advise her. If the daughter is interested and ambitious, she will absorb quickly what she needs to know. In other words, once a daughter is considered as a successor, all rules regarding successors apply to her.

Women and Communication

Most family problems start with inadequate communication. A daughter in business may rely on the same communications techniques she ordinarily uses to achieve personal favor from her parents. She may be termed "bitchy" or "nagging" by other siblings and employees while the same traits in her brother(s) are seen as "forcefulness" and "following up on details." The basic problem here is that the technique the daughter is using is emotionally based. If a request is not granted, her reaction is anger or pouting. In business, this type of display can foster an unstable work atmosphere. It demoralizes employees and encourages them to react in a similar way to gain their ends.

Communications skills can be learned. The rationalization, "That is just the way she is and you'll never change her" is not true when it comes to learning to communicate. Culturally, most women have been taught to express themselves with tears, pleading, and petulance. In fact, they are expected to do so. As more of them enter the business world, they are retraining themselves to show their basic leadership qualities in a way devoid of these gender expectations.

Families try to compensate daughters in many ways for not going into the business. If the family message is equality, then the daughter will be given property in equal value to the son's share in the business. This can be frustrating to a talented young woman with an interest in the family enterprise. The side message here is that she will be taken care of because she is not competent to work for money. Depending on her personality, this daughter may squander her inheritance because she has little understanding of how it was earned. On the other hand, it may be a constant reminder to her of what she perceives as her lack of ability. In this case, she may become miserly with her money and is an easy prey to the alcohol, drug, and psychological problems related to low self-esteem and feelings of inadequacy.

Another daughter might underwrite a business for her husband that she is interested in herself. She is thrilled by his ideas and, because of her exposure to her family's business, understands how they can be implemented. Yet, she is reluctant to accept a managerial role in the business because of her family's hidden message that she is unqualified.

Some families "handle" their wives' and daughters' ambitions by giving them a task related to the family business. These women may be asked to decorate offices, consult with architects on building programs, or stage elaborate social affairs. The talent it takes to do these things successfully demonstrates that the woman has organizational skills that are being ignored.

Any job a woman is asked to do for the family business that parallels a professional field should be recognized as such. The wife or daughter who enjoys executing these tasks is a professional asset to the company. Recognition of her ability, adequate compensation, and consideration as a successor should be forthcoming.

The "Family Business Wife": Lillian Harwood

Not every woman whose husband heads a family business will want to participate in it directly. She may prefer to reflect the family philosophy in a private setting, subordinating her own personality to the traditions of the family and the beliefs of the husband. She is an extension of his "perfection." Still another type prefers total anonymity, both in the community and in the business. She finds it too difficult to balance her business and her personal lives. In the case of the husband's death, both of these women will have enormous difficulty adjusting to corporate ownership and are likely to sell the company or give it away.

Lillian Harwood was one such woman. Unlike Melinda Oakton, she was a family business wife, not a corporate one. The difference between the family business wife and the corporate wife is *who sets the rules*. The family business wife reflects her husband and a tradition, which both may change as they see fit. In an ordinary corporation, the executive wife must conform to the image of the company despite its contradictions with her own personality. In addition, she is asked to uproot herself at any time to follow her husband. The corporate family is related by a series of common objectives and any member can be replaced at any time. In a family business, the common ground is the trust and love within the family for its members and their continued growth. It's hard to replace a family member.

Lillian Harwood understood her husband's concept of the business, and she had absorbed many skills from being at her husband's side. When Charles, the heir Louis casually designated, refused to head the company, Lillian was at a loss. Her expertise and desire were not in operating Harwood E&C. Yet, in her mind the business was integral to family unity. If it was sold, the family would be separated from something important to all of them.

Lillian Harwood helped to orchestrate the succession by her insistence on facing the issue despite Louis's objections. The two dominant Harwood family messages—"Family is important" and "Never give up"—worked for Lillian in a time of crisis. Louis's happiness was important to her, but she did not want to think this meant selling family tradition or separating from her children over business matters. When it became clear to her that Louis would not make the necessary moves to ensure the future of the business, she initiated the process. Louis was able to "save face" in this situation because of his illness. Wives who initiate the succession question are confronted with the sensitivity of the issue for their husbands and often abandon the idea. The resultant worry and frustration places a great strain on the marriage.

Another type of wife and mother inherits control of the family business. She dispenses power as a way of manipulating her children. She may have learned this from her predecessor, or it may be a part of her personality. In either case, it is detrimental to all involved. The object of the business is to make profits and any other purpose cheats all family members of this goal.

Great battles go on in family businesses where control of family members' lives is the key issue. The only people who profit are the lawyers, accountants, and others hired by family members to represent their interests and perpetuate the problem. Few businesses have profits to share after these lengthy internecine wars.

Breaking with the Past

In addition to the emotional baggage a wife or daughter must handle in the family business, she shares the same problems of other working women with families. She must juggle schedules and supply quality time to her children, her husband, and herself. Not every woman has the capability or wish to do this. Without a strong desire to participate in the business, she may fail to overcome these "obstacles." Any woman entering the business world must do so with an open eye to the demands it makes on time and energy. She must form a clear image of herself in a business role. This image is essential to her future success.

As the woman gains skill and experience, acceptance by employees and peers will be forthcoming. The business climate toward women is changing rapidly. Only in certain generational or social situations do women now find themselves viewed as women first and foremost. Any successful businessperson knows the value of a talented employee. If that employee is contributing toward the profits of the company, gender will cease to be a major problem.

This does not mean that the battle for equal pay for equal work has been won. The problem of compensation for work in a family business is a sticky one at best. Some families pay members too much for too little work. Others fail to pay family members enough, especially the women. As the company's management is professionalized, one of the issues to be considered is pay in line with skill, experience, and the nature of the job. Gender and family relationship are not the major considerations. Such a policy works to enhance everyone's self-image. In effect, people know their relative worth because they are paid fair market salaries in keeping with their contribution.

The Harwoods, with all the problems they exhibited, gave the family business priority. This meant breaking with outmoded ideas and moving the business toward a professional status. The daughter and wife became central, not peripheral figures in the survival of the company. If all family businesses listened to the Harwood message, they could profit. Wives and daughters must not be overlooked on any level. The family business that recognizes this expands its potential immediately.

7

In-Laws and Outlaws

In addition to wives and daughters, other family members often have to prove their worth to enter the family business. In-laws are many times considered the outlaws of family enterprise. In addition to making themselves a part of a family unit, these men and women face the issue of whether or not they will be invited into the family company.

Someone who marries into a family with a business tradition is usually expected to follow the path of other, same-sex members of the family. If they are active in the business, a place will be found for the in-law. Problems arise in the event the in-law does not want to participate in the enterprise. The reluctance to do so for whatever reason makes the in-law an outlaw.

In contrast, the new in-law may want to play an equal part in the business but may not have the skills or the background to do so. This case can be handled in the same way as with any unskilled family member. The new in-law can receive training for whatever position is appropriate. If the training is ineffective or if no talent for the job is demonstrated, a delicate situation arises. In this situation, the family must have clear communications channels. It also needs to install sound business practices so that the in-law understands that he must demonstrate competency to be given a position.

A special type of "in-law" is the second, younger wife of the company founder. His children may see her as a threat to their continuance in the business. This may be so if the entrepreneur does not make provisions for succession and, in fact, leaves her his shares of the company.

One way to handle this problem is for the entrepreneur to have an agreement with the second wife concerning her share and participation in the business after his death. This must be a formal, written contract that clearly states his intentions. She must be aware of all the ramifications of it and be a willing cosigner to its provisions. It will save a lot of wear and tear on the family unity, in both the present and the future.

Strained Relationships

In-laws are often judged more harshly than other family members in terms of job performance. Therefore, the job description and the in-law must fit together. Then, the in-law has an idea of what is expected of him. He knows, and the family knows, whether or not he is qualified for the position. Parents may want the daughter to live well and compensate the son-in-law beyond his abilities. When this occurs, in the business, he will be seen as a buffoon without portfolio. In-laws who come into the business must meet the criteria for the job for the health and happiness of all family members, and, most important, themselves.

In-laws face other problems that encourage strained relationships. Parents may not always accept the new family member because of social, religious, or financial reasons. Or they may simply think no one is good enough for their child. The in-law who takes part in the family business may never get the opportunity to prove his worth.

Elaine worked during her first pregnancy. It was a busy, happy time for her. Everything was going her way. She was concerned about her husband's increased dependence on alcohol to relieve his "stress," but the relationship continued to go well from her point of view. She did not give Robert's problem the attention it demanded. Two years later, when their son was born, the marriage was in serious trouble.

The Harwood message "Family is important" did not allow Elaine to give up on her marriage. She thought Robert could cope with his alcohol problem, and she wanted to help him but not interfere. However, when the problem spilled over into the community—when Robert was arrested for driving while intoxicated—Elaine decided to take charge. She recognized its implications for the future.

There are other twists. One daughter-in-law came to work in the business and was very successful. Difficulties came up in her marriage, and she divorced the son. She was asked to stay in her job because she was thoroughly professional. In fact, the father kicked the son out of the business because he was not professional.

In another case, two children of a wealthy entrepreneur had unexpected experiences because of their spouses. The son married a social climber. He was extravagant with his money and the two of them spent beyond their means. The father disliked his son's living style but continued to advance him money to cover his expenses. The daughter married a prudent, talented man with a portfolio of business experience. He entered the family business, did his homework, and became a valued employee.

The father had intended to leave the business equally to his two children. But when his daughter developed a crippling illness, the father changed his mind. He knew his son would squander everything in a short time, and his daughter would never be able to adequately manage her part of the business because of her disability. He therefore provided for both children, but left the business control to his son-in-law. It proved to be a difficult but wise decision. The son-in-law brought the business to its greatest heights, and all family members benefited by his efforts.

Sometimes a son-in-law is given the job that should go to the daughter. She, in turn, is placed in a lesser job and may be very unhappy. This will cause a strain on their personal relationship and an attitudinal problem within the business. Again, the family needs to institute good communications systems to keep in touch with the wishes of all its members.

The In-Law Outlawed: Robert Harwood

Elaine Harwood's marriage did not fail because Robert was not taken into the Harwood family business. But the fact did contribute to their overall marital problems. Louis ignored Robert as a potential employee, because he was not confident in his ability. This was true. Robert's self-confidence problems predated his marriage to Elaine and would not have survived her success regardless of the Harwood business.

A creative and ambitious woman, Elaine set out to be a success. Her observations of her father over many years, the lessons at the dinner table, the many questions he answered for her—this information contributed to the achievement of her business goals. Only in her marriage did Elaine come face to face with the unsolved problems associated with her father.

Robert was a manufacturing representative when Elaine met him. He was charming and attractive. On the surface, he mirrored her father's confidence. Robert's constant attention through gifts and flowers pleased and flattered her. Elaine was a striking woman with a unique fashion style and personality that made her in demand socially. When she entered a room, heads turned at her presence. She exuded warmth and strength. However, her ambition took precedence over thoughts of marriage and family.

In the first few weeks after their meeting, Robert pursued Elaine openly. She liked his attention and felt a strange sense of power when she realized this successful young man was falling in love with her. She was actually more important than his business, or so he made her think.

As her own business prospered, Elaine became increasingly annoyed by her parents' persistent questions about marriage. She loved her family and never questioned the idea that she would marry eventually. When Robert proposed, she accepted, as much to please her parents as herself. In the very complicated way families have of rationalizing and interacting, Elaine hoped to have her father's approval of her marriage partner, but she also wanted someone who would understand her ambition.

Louis and Lillian liked Robert personally and welcomed him into the family. Both silently hoped he would encourage Elaine to have children and gradually remove herself from business. As it became evident that Robert was not going to do so, both parents began to find fault with him. In addition, Robert's career rivalry with Elaine entered the picture. Elaine's business was given a sudden boost when she landed a corporate contract. His own career was given a jolt when the company he worked for was sold. A new management structure gave him little room for promotion.

Elaine waited for her father to invite Robert into the Harwood business. It was apparent to her that Louis had to consider a successor. Robert had many of her father's talents, and she believed he could make a valuable contribution to the company. In a vague way, she pictured herself and Robert eventually running the family business.

Louis perceived Robert differently. He saw him as weak because he had failed to persuade Elaine to limit her goals to a family. Also, he correctly saw Robert as being comfortable in a secondary role, and not wanting the full responsibility for a company. The issue of Robert entering the Harwood business was never openly discussed. To Elaine, her father had simply ignored Robert's abilities as well as hers.

This complicated interaction between father and daughter added to Robert's career frustration, and his drinking increased. The birth of their first child, a daughter, did little to bolster his sense of confidence. He felt trapped by circumstances and the success of Elaine's business.

Louis Harwood had always been a social drinker, sometimes indulging himself heavily. However, he was never incapacitated by alcohol to the point where he could not meet his obligations. Further, he never made a "fool" of himself in public. Because of his own "control," Louis had little empathy for Robert's problem. He encouraged Elaine's decision to divorce Robert after her efforts to enter him in a rehabilitation program failed. Robert's personal frustrations about his future, his envy of his wife's success, and his sense of rejection by his in-laws was more than he could handle. His self-confidence had never been as strong as his surface behavior indicated. Now it was crushed, and he was depressed.

Elaine's divorce focused on her success as much as it did on Robert's alcohol problem. The divorce cost her in financial terms, but she gained custody of the children and quickly put the past behind her—as far as Robert was concerned.

Elaine suffered for Robert's deficiencies in several ways. She had always tried to be perfect in her father's eyes. Her "dreadful mistake with Robert," as she termed it, tarnished her own self-image. The relationship that developed between her and her father during the divorce year added a complication she was not prepared to accept. Her father accepted her mistake, and she was still angry with him! Elaine had not dealt openly with her competitiveness with Louis or with her anger at being rejected by him for a role in the company. Instead, she focused the anger outwardly, on her marriage. She found herself apologizing to her father for Robert's mistakes.

The In-Law Admitted: Andrew Oakton

The Lake-Oakton example stands in sharp contrast to Elaine and Robert. Melinda and Andrew defined the issues clearly and decided to fight for what they wanted. They were prepared to lose both money and favor if her father did not give them the prerequisite authority for the son-in-law, Andrew, to succeed. At the same time, Melinda never let up on her determination to communicate with her father and foster a platform of understanding between him and her husband.

In the beginning, Andrew encountered a problem that many in-laws face: failure to read the family messages correctly. In-laws may begin to participate in ways that other family members resent. They may be following the family "rules" without understanding the underlying family message. Andrew was asked to come into the business and prepare himself to eventually be its sole operator. What he did not understand was that Charlie had no intention of giving control to him immediately, and the resultant difficulty led to Andrew leaving the company. The family message must be brought into line with business goals.

In the end, Charlie Lake understood he was not losing his business, but that he gained a strong, competent son-in-law who could carry on the family tradition and give his daughter what Charlie felt she should have.

Andrew's lifelong dream had been to operate a business like the one Charlie owned. At the end of his first year heading Charlie's company, Andrew concluded that the business was financially secure—so solid, in fact, that it was possible to draw off significant capital for other investment purposes. In no way would this jeopardize the financial position of the parent organization.

Andrew began to devise a comprehensive plan for the creation of a wholly-owned subsidiary devoted to investments. A strategy was outlined and people were employed to implement it. The plan was and remains very successful. The company's additional financial interest has increased the profits to all family members.

Many in-law problems can be solved by attention to good business and communications practices. Some cannot. In any case, the family must separate the emotional issues and operate the business in an organized, predictable way. The provisions made for all family members must be in keeping with the goals and tradition of the business. Clear rules for entry into the company are essential. Competence, not bloodline, is the important qualification. A family needs to define what it means by "taking care" of its members. That should not mean it is destroying them emotionally, and the future of the family business in the process.

8

Substance Abuse

In November 1984, the son of a Texas tycoon went on trial for the premeditated murder of his father. The motive, charged the prosecutor, was "greed and money." The half-sister of the defendant said he freebased cocaine as a part of his drug-using lifestyle. This scenario might sound like a Grade B movie, but it is a real-life example of the difficulty drug and alcohol abuse presents to a family and its business interests.

Not all families who encounter substance abuse end up in as extreme a situation as this Texas family. But drugs do make a difference, whether or not the law becomes involved. The family that has a drug abuse problem in its midst will suffer privately and publicly. The family loses its self-respect, and the business forfeits the opportunity to expand to its fullest potential.

"It's None of My Business"

Substance abuse is pervasive in today's business community. Some public corporations have programs to help employees deal with this problem. Others fire employees regardless of tenure or talent. Owners and managers have realized how easily the company's profits can fall when employees are dependent on alcohol, marijuana, cocaine, amphetamines, and over-the-counter drugs.

In a family business the problem is compounded because of close personal relationships and the perceived stigma of admitting a problem within its ranks. Alcohol seems to have a genetic and social base that the family is unwilling to face. Recreational drinking is an accepted relaxant for many families. The person who imbibes too much is dismissed as "just having a good time." As long as a person appears to do his job—whether the drinking occurs in the morning, at noon, at the cocktail hour, or beyond—people react with "It's none of my business." However, when drinking complicates a person's relationships with others, the family must realize that the person *is* an abuser of alcohol and thus an alcoholic. For this individual, alcohol use has ceased to become a leisure-time indulgence. *It is now a form of suicide.* The same is true of any addictive substance.

Everything that enters the body affects it in some way. But alcohol and drugs affect the brain especially quickly and can cause impairment of functioning in a short time. Permanent disabilities can result from the use and abuse of alcohol and drugs. The business executive who seems quite "straight" or sober may actually be significantly disabled in his decision making. This kind of loss jeopardizes the resources and opportunities of the entire enterprise and the fates of all those people—owners, managers, employees, customers, creditors, and so on—who are intertwined with the business.

It is difficult to attribute a disastrous business decision to a substance-related disorder. The consequences of apparently simple actions or choices—failure to perceive a specific opportunity or alternative, failure to ask a key question, failure to return a telephone call on time, or failure to consult with others—do not reveal themselves directly. In fact, failures that result directly from a substance-related disability may never become obvious.

In addition, only a few people may be in a position to directly perceive, recognize, or comment on the performance of a family business member. If the observer is not a family member, it may be difficult to bring the problem to the attention of the family. In this way, the problem goes untreated.

Alcohol in the Family: The Harwoods Revealed

The Harwoods ignored the problem in their ranks. Louis Harwood stayed out of his elder son's personal life. When Charles's appearance began to reflect his abuse problem, Louis simply overlooked it. Charles was more than just his son; he represented the deceased brother and confidant whom Louis had also protected. Louis had explained away his brother's behavior simply as eccentric and erratic. It had not mattered because Louis always had control of the business decisions. And he had never allowed his son Charles to make a really important decision. Why, then, should he tell him how to dress or act? Louis was comfortable with this rationalization. On the other hand, it contributed subconsciously to his unwillingness to make plans for a successor.

There is also the question of what is and what is not considered excessive substance abuse. In Charles Harwood's case, he *did* come into the office and he did function during some of the day with efficiency. But he did not have any real responsibilities, so his impact on the business was not as great from a profit point of view as it was from a psychological point of view. Employees just worked around him when he was "under the weather."

Louis Harwood had always used alcohol as a relaxant and as a business-social tool. He had many three-martini lunches and sometimes imbibed heavily after hours. If he occasionally took a day off to "rest," no one regarded it as a recuperative period from anything except overwork. What Louis did was to set up a precedent for alcohol use in the business and in his family life. This was the example he presented to his children as "okay" for them to follow. Therefore, he could not speak to Charles about his "problem," nor did he see it as a problem.

Elaine overlooked the potential difficulty she would have with Robert because she assumed he would handle alcohol as her father did. Elaine's marriage to Robert illustrates recent research findings that the children of those who abuse alcohol tend to marry alcoholics or persons predisposed to alcohol-related problems. Although Louis, Sr. never manifested an alcohol addiction, it is possible that he would have developed a problem with alcohol if his health condition had not precipitated changes in diet and alcohol consumption.

Elaine's father saw Robert as weak because he could not control alcohol. But more than that, Louis lost respect for Robert because he had allowed his use of alcohol to become so obsessive that his behavior in the community reflected badly on the Harwood family.

Neither Louis or Elaine thought of giving up social drinking because Robert could not handle it. For her part, Lillian was quite dependent on cough-and-cold medications, which contained depressants for sleep, and on other over-the-counter products. These too constitute a psychological dependency when used regularly. Only high blood pressure made Louis stop drinking, and Elaine cut down on her social drinking because she became very health-minded. When Charles's substance problems surfaced, the entire family became conscious of the effect of alcohol and drugs in their lives. They came to understand these drugs as masking communication from their bodies and, in a larger sense, as deflecting interpersonal communication among them.

The Harwood attitude toward addictive substances is typical of many families who protect their members until their behavior becomes so aberrant or dangerous as to demand a legal response. At that point, the authority of the individual is isolated by other family members if at all possible. However, if the substance abuser heads the company, the problem becomes extremely complicated.

The "False Bookcase": Jeff Franklin

Jeff Franklin was the owner and director of a large business that manufactured equipment for construction purposes. There were more than 300 employees in his company. The business environment was highly volatile and visible to the public eye. Three of the six top directors of the company were Jeff's two sons and his wife. Jeff was not particularly dominant in the business. His directors, all foxes and wolves in their own right, were cleverly managing the day-to-day affairs of the business. The two sons were in many ways indistinguishable from the other directors, who were absorbed into Jeff's family culture rather than remaining distinct as nonfamily members. This alone seeded problems for the business, but it was the executive family's behavior that was the real problem.

The entire executive family drank, but not to such excess as to come to public notice or to affect the reputation, power, position, or physical health of any one director. It was *where* and *when* they drank that became dangerous to the stability of the company.

Every afternoon at five o'clock, as the majority of employees were leaving the parking lot, the directors filed into Jeff's office and settled comfortably into their chairs around the conference table, with Jeff presiding from his capacious leather throne. They loosened their ties and began to talk about operations, personnel, and futures. Jeff would open the false bookcase, remove glasses, ice, and liquor specific to the tastes of each director, and ritually pass the drinks around.

It was there and then that the important, but subtle,

internecine battles were waged and major decisions made. Enemies were identified and decried, strategies for revenge were devised, and irremedial actions were taken—all after fatigue, privacy, and alcohol had taken their toll of cautious judgment. When these ill-based plans became public, the very continuance of the firm was threatened. As demands were made for apologies and resignations, Jeff stood behind his "family" to the last, vociferously defending policies and actions whose genesis and purpose he could not for his life recall. Only through enormous effort on the part of management and the directors was the firm able to retain its strong market position. The afternoon "directors' meetings" came to an abrupt end.

Wine Before Sales: Foster Ellison

Foster Ellison, his wife, and two other partners ran a highly successful and rapidly expanding telecommunications business. He was the sole, adopted son of an upper-middle-income family in which drinking was a routine part of evening and weekend sociability. He attended a Big Ten university and joined a fraternity, where he acquired a reputation as a heavy but not problem drinker. He carried his pattern of drinking and sociability into the competitive business world, negotiating and concluding major sales agreements in the warmth of good restaurants and mellow wines.

As the firm grew, his drinking did not appear to impair his ability to direct the course of the business and maintain control over his partners' activities. It also did not impair his ability to put in sixteen-hour days for weeks on end and to commute routinely across the country, although the quality of his work and of his private life became questionable to his family. (In the business, the partners were required to accept new roles, tasks, and methods during the period of expansion, and then to adjust to a period of economic retrenchment characterized by intense competition and the bankrupcy of comparable businesses.) Long periods of work, uninterrupted by play or holidays, in combination with growing conflicts among the partners, resulted in a serious attack of hypertension for Foster.

Foster's wife dealt with the physical disability by increasing his life insurance—not by insisting that Foster alter his lifestyle or seek medical care. Startled by this pragmatic attitude, Foster sought medical advice, which included a rigid diet, shorter work hours, regular naps, and an end to both smoking and drinking. Initially, his colleagues perceived this spartan existence as a threat. Foster had become "different," and his choice of foods and nonalcoholic drinks was translated as a rebuke to them. It took months for his personal and business lives to become sorted out. It also took time for his family, partners, associates, and clients to alter their image and expectations of him and to accept his changed identity.

Is Alcoholism Inherited?

Alcohol dependency explains many business behaviors. Alcohol pervades all decision and communications systems, and compounds other problems endemic to the business. It is often used to sanction personal and corporate irresponsibility. However, it is unlikely that other family members, partners, employees, or customers will accept alcohol as an excuse for the continuance of irresponsible business behavior. Genetic and biochemical explanations portray alcoholism as beyond individual control. That these factors are significant in the treatment sense, however, does not give them merit in the business world, where the behaviors are so threatening.

Alcoholism is not randomly distributed throughout a population. It is not like a virus that anyone and everyone in a population is equally likely to contract. Many studies have suggested that there are specific subpopulations that are "predisposed" to or "at greater risk" of developing an alcohol problem. Acknowledging these preceding conditions does not excuse the constellation of self-destructive behaviors displayed

95

by alcoholics, since there is no evidence that alcohol use is not subject to one's own volition and the volition of the members of one's family and social world.

The role of the family is critical in the "inheritance" of alcohol risk. Family provides a series of predisposing bases, including genetic inheritance, familial and cultural drinking patterns, personality, fetal alcohol syndrome, psychopathology, and physiological functioning. It is important to recognize these relationships and their effect on personal and business fates. For example, the ingestion of alcohol is likely to damage, through toxic and organic effects, particular mental functions and to result, in the children of alcoholics, in both a predisposition to alcohol use and some brain damage. Thus, in two generations of the same family, the capacity to manage alcohol and to think may be seriously impaired. The cumulative consequences of two or more generations with such disability on business decision making is likely to be profound.

The role of genetic factors in alcoholism occupies a prominent place in the journals and conventions of the professions that research and treat alcoholism. It also occupies a prominent place in the "politics" of the alcoholism treatment industry. The suggestion that alcoholism is an unavoidable disease embedded in one's genetic inheritance is often seen to remove the individual's responsibility for the drinking behavior, a responsibility that lies at the heart of certain forms of alcohol treatment. It also suggests to some alcoholics that they should wait for a magic pill or other genetic tool to cure their disease (as other diseases have been defeated in the past) rather than take immediate action and assume the responsibility of altering their own behaviors.

Many genetic studies suggest that alcoholism is not inherited in the same way as grandfather's nose, but that what is inherited is a predisposition—a risk—for developing alcohol problems or for being especially vulnerable to the effects of alcohol. There may be a physiological basis; alcoholics may have a body chemistry that inhibits the normal processing of alcohol in their systems. Research up to now has not indicated the existence of an "alcoholism gene," an aberration in the DNA that causes a person to become alcoholic. However, the likelihood that a child will develop alcoholism in later life is correlated with alcoholism in the biological parents.

In addition to being at higher risk of alcoholism than are the children of nonalcoholic fathers, the children of alcoholic fathers tend to have a greater tolerance for alcohol, to appear less intoxicated, to have fewer body reactions to alcohol, to report fewer feelings of intoxication, and to show less change in the ability to coordinate movements after drinking a certain amount of alcohol than are the children of nonalcoholic fathers.

More severe problems with alcohol tend to occur when a person has several relatives and generations of relatives exhibiting alcoholism. Whether this tendency is due more to environmental than to genetic influences is still quite uncertain among researchers. There is little doubt that a person exposed to a social environment in which heavy drinking is the custom and alcohol is highly available will have a much greater chance of developing alcoholism than a person lacking such predisposing factors. However, while they must be more guarded in their relationship to alcohol, they are not "predetermined" to become alcoholics. Neither genetic inheritance nor alcoholic environments—nor the combination of the two—has been found to be "deterministic." Children of alcoholics, embedded in alcohol-prone families, often do not drink, for whatever reasons, even though their chances of developing alcoholism are statistically higher than those of people who have no such genetic or social background.

The "Adopted Family Member"

Alcoholism is the result of many factors, choices, relationships, and behaviors built up over a long period of time, some of which preceded the birth of the identified alcoholic. It is rare for alcohol abuse, drug abuse, or other addictions to appear in only one member of a family or in one generation. It is not uncommon to find genograms like that in Figure 6.

Typically, alcohol is an "old member" of both sides of the family, with a long and honored cultural, social, and familial tradition. Family here means more than the nuclear family. It also means the intergenerational family structure, extended kinship, and multiple family systems. Further, the substance of choice to which people become addicted is not necessarily

Figure 6. Message genogram of an alcoholic family.

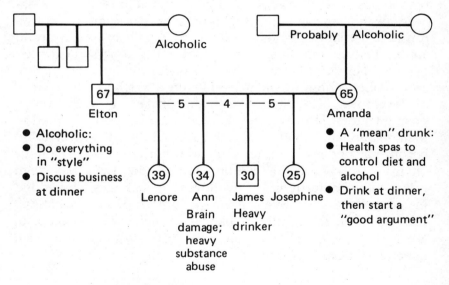

Family Messages

- Tolerate alcoholism and substance abuse.
- Indulge children.
- Maintain interpersonal distance.
- Submerge feelings.

specific to the family. Addiction to alcohol, heroin, marijuana, cocaine, sleeping pills, tobacco, or food is dependent on one's social style, the availability of the substance, and the peer practice of each generation within a family. *It is the addictive behavior itself, rather than the substance, that is embedded in families.*

Alcoholism is often treated as if it were a visible injury or disease borne by one family member only, like a cancer. It is spoken about in whispers and only on occasion, accompanied by wistful sighs and helpless shrugs. But alcoholism is far more than the personal tribulation of one individual. It is like an adopted family member, with a personality, roles, and rewards all its own. At the same time, it is a vital influence on every other family member. What, then, is this "adopted person" like? What does "he" do to family communications, relationships, and business? What keeps "him" embedded within the family business, and what is the cost of getting rid of "him"?

Before alcoholism was viewed as a social, psychological, or medical disease, alcohol was often personified as if it had a character and will separate from that of the drinking person. The personifications are still part of our everyday language—"demon rum," "the devil in the bottle," "that's the alcohol talking," and "he's under the influence." Alcohol, as a new "human" presence, becomes a family member, a confidant, a companion, and a business associate. It is included in the social scene on many, or even all, family occasions. Room is made for alcohol in the board room, dining room, and bedroom. Personal relationships, social relationships, and power relationships are all reorganized to make room for the newcomer, within both nuclear and extended families.

This adopted family member is not easy to incorporate. It is demanding, insistent, insidious, reckless, risk-taking, forgetful, and moody—alternating rapidly among melancholy, sociability, depression, conviviality, and outrage. It is also theatrically and falsely insightful and honest *(in vino veritas)*. Perhaps the most dangerous characteristic of alcohol is that it cannot seem to function in a world of vital personal and business communications. Its messages are often undecipherable, inconsistent, untrustworthy, and impermanent. It is a poor receiver of messages, so that family members and business associates do not know whether, when, or how their messages have been received and acknowledged. Finally, alcohol is a poor conduit of messages from one member or one time period to another.

The way in which families accommodate is by routing communications over, around, and beneath this member, building new arrangements in which, though alcohol may lie at the center, family and business actions occur around the periphery, through new conduits and power arrangements.

The Infantilized Alcoholic: Richard Beser

Despite a deceptive façade of noninvolvement, family members are covertly enmeshed in sticky, ambivalent ties and tend to unwittingly keep an alcoholic family member in an inappropriately dependent position, to infantilize him, to perceive him as weak, and to encourage him to escape frustrations rather than overcome them. In this way, families act in collusion to perpetuate substance use. This collusion may take the form of only token concern with alcoholism or even active support of the drinking behavior.

The Beser family case incorporates most of these problems. The Besers owned a chain of upscale men's and women's specialty stores. Edward Beser and his wife, Elizabeth, had a very organized family life. They were always willing to take responsibility for family gatherings, especially at holiday time. Edward's brother, Richard, resented his brother always "taking charge" and retaliated by becoming drunk at all family functions. Richard's attitude was shared by his wife, Darla, who was his drinking partner. Finally, the communication between the two families became impossible to maintain with any degree of civility.

When time came for a successor to be chosen for the family business, Edward fulfilled the criteria for the job and was chosen. This was the final blow to Richard's ego, and he moved his family to another state. His parents were very unhappy about the circumstances, and the elder Beser became very depressed about the "break" in the family. Edward tried to establish a communication with his brother, but Richard's alcohol problem denied it. When the children were no longer allowed to visit their grandparents—to punish them in Richard's eyes for having chosen his brother to run the company— the elder Beser had a stroke. All family members blamed Richard for the event and cut off communication with him and his family. Further, he was denied revenues from the company, both by his father's will and by his brother.

Richard's drinking continued to increase, as did his anger and guilt. He and Darla began to fight, and the children became increasingly disturbed by their parents' erratic behavior. One day in a drunken rage, Richard hit his son so hard that the child's eye was permanently damaged. Soon after, beside himself with guilt and depression, Richard jumped into his car and drove frantically away. The accident that occurred a short time later was deemed just that, but his wife and other family members were never certain he had not committed suicide.

Treatment efforts for addicts of all kinds are often based on "unlearning" destructive behavior and altering patterns of social reinforcement. The greater the number of reinforcing members, the more difficult it is to change basic patterns. Change involves major shifts in power allocation and reward systems and demands new forms of communication. This kind of change is revolutionary in the most political sense of the word. Thus, assigning blame to the drinking member, in the unlikely event that there be just one, is not a very profitable exercise. Focus must be placed on the entire social system that supports and derives rewards from the addictive behavior.

A recovering alcoholic may have to confront an entire array of deteriorated conditions—divorce or marital estrangement, financial ruin, career crisis, legal entanglement, health problems, social dislocations, and so on. The family has chosen to deal with the drinking member in one way. The changed member will be a displaced person within a network of social subsystems, each of which has progressively modified its stance, as alcohol became more critical to his role and functioning.

The recovering "problem carrier" in the family and the family-owned business may want to reoccupy the powerful, influential, and central roles that are now occupied by others. These others may even encourage the return of alcoholism, the complete reincorporation of the substance into family and business life, in order to ensure the status quo of power, position, rewards, and communications.

The problem of drugs includes all of the above and, in addition, their illegality. Consequently, when a family member becomes a heavy user, and purchases more illegal substances as dependency grows, the chances of his getting caught by the authorities increases. If such a "bust" takes place, the entire family and its business comes under scrutiny by the government authorities and the public alike. In many businesses, this type of publicity can be disastrous. Also, a family member who finds himself in this position may view suicide or desertion as the only way out.

Cocaine off the Books: Ron Nedham

Ron and Jan Nedham owned a small consulting firm. Their children were part-time employees and small equity owners. Ron and Jan were equally intelligent and aggressive in business affairs. However, Ron took responsibility for handling the firm's financial affairs and lucrative contracts. Jan managed the production end as well as all the support functions. Ron and Jan were so overwhelmed by creating products and maintaining information networks that they decided to assign all personal and corporate accounting and tax work to an external accountant. Because of their high income and rapid cash flow, there was always enough money to meet current expenses. Fiscal panic was intermittent, usually coinciding with having to "front end" the costs of large new projects and having to sort out annual tax confusion upon handing receipts in a shoebox to the accountant.

Jan was so busy with her responsibilities that she did not investigate why their standard of living was relatively low in view of the large billings of the company. Nonetheless, Ron impulsively made major financial commitments, such as buying computer equipment and taking out a new, larger mortgage, from the commingled family and business accounts, assuring Jan that her signature was a formality and the accounts were sound.

One day, a friend and close associate was helping Ron prepare a major, overdue report. As he struggled to keep Ron's attention focused on the product, a young, well-dressed man entered the office unannounced. Ron opened the middle drawer of his desk, removed a small packet of money, ostentatiously counted out ten $1,000 bills, and handed them to the stranger. The man then handed Ron a fat plastic bag of cocaine and left. Ron immediately went through the ritual of preparing and snorting "a couple of lines." His friend, aware of Ron's drug use but surprised by Ron's blatant actions, said simply, "I hope that makes you alert enough to finish this damned report!" It didn't.

A few weeks later Ron moved out of his home, abandoned the business, and disappeared to another city, avoiding contact with family, friends, and associates. His accountant had discovered a crippling personal and corporate tax liability and almost total depletion of business assets (of which the cocaine was not a calculated inventory item). The outstanding business and mortgage costs threatened to swamp the family's remaining resources, which no longer included a husband, father, business partner, and cocaine addict.

Working Toward Solutions

These brief depictions highlight the costs to businesses of alcohol- and drug-altered decision making and the costs to families of such disasters and near disasters. The incorporation and sanctioning of drinking and drug use in regular business life generates important risks for both families and businesses.

The issue here is not drinking or drugs per se. If it were, the obvious solution would be to conduct business only when all parties were sober or free of drugs. Far more important is the damaging effect of alcohol and drugs on human communications systems. The decisions made by Jeff Franklin's executives had an attenuated grounding in reality, a reality clouded by alcohol. Ron Nedham's covert habits completely destroyed his business, family, and wealth. By choosing a new behavior, Foster Ellison lost the support system that had enabled him to continue his hard-driving, heavy drinking ways; communicating his new identity and building a support system for it were almost as draining as continuing his previous workaholic role, so difficult, in fact, that he seriously considered giving up his new regimen.

The family communications system and the business communications system not only interact but act as one. In order to make effective and appropriate family business decisions, it is essential that the communications system clearly transmit factual matters, personal relations, and other "messages."

The effects of alcohol on these communications systems are in no way limited to the period of time whan a family member is "under the influence." The long-term abuse of substances can effectively stymie the ability to transmit, recognize, receive, translate, retain, recall, and utilize information of any kind. Alcohol can also cause a person's internal communications system to be seriously and permanently impaired. The person may no longer be able to communicate accurately or effectively with himself about internal relationships or relationships with the people, objects, and conditions in his external world.

Helping such a person go through substance withdrawal is not a simple task. Nor is it the time to make vital changes in family and business communications. A person undergoing short-term and long-term withdrawal may suffer hypoglycemia, weakness, gastric distress, nausea, anoxia, central nervous system and autonomic system disorganization, excessive perspiration, tremors, disorientation, mental anguish and confusion, sleep disturbance, perceptual defects, personality distortions, hallucinations, and elevated rates of temperature, blood pressure, and heart rate. (Just reading the syndrome of problems is overwhelming.) The intensity of these problems attests, as little else can, to the degree of dependency the body and mind develop for alcohol and other drugs.

In addition to physical and emotional disorders, there are psychosocial consequences. The individual loses personal integrity and honesty, has increased intolerance to stress, loses impulse control, and experiences memory defects and losses, ramblings, blackouts, lack of insight, fear, resentment, depression, paranoia, and loss of stamina. Can you imagine yourself hiring or retaining an individual who was exhibiting these behaviors and, further, putting that person in a decision-making position—say, at the heart of the business? How would you communicate with that person through the haze of cognitive failure, infantile attitudes, dishonesty, and mood swings?

It is of paramount importance that businesses be conducted by adults. Drinking and drug-using family members are not functioning as adults in their private, family, and business lives. Mere freedom from addiction does not necessarily imply an adult state. Such independence may mean only pseudo-adult functioning, an aping or imitation of adulthood, whether by individuals or by entire families. To the degree that nonsubstance-abusing members do not alter their reward systems from reliance on negative behaviors, they too are embedding

105

inappropriate destructive elements into the foundations of family-owned businesses.

"Booze and Build": The Moser Dynasty

Families can conquer the alcohol and substance abuse behaviors that threaten them and their businesses, even when the problem is long-standing. The Moser family is a case in point. The Mosers own and operate a heavy construction business. They build bridges and hard road surfaces. The substance abuse problem, like the business itself, spans three generations.

The grandfather, Herman Moser, was a shrewd businessman. During World War II he took a small road construction firm and quickly built it into a multimillion-dollar enterprise. Herman's expertise and macho "drink until dawn and get the job done" image made him a colorful character in his state. Federal and state procurement agents had a hard time resisting Herman's repartee and "bring this man another drink" hospitality. His nickname, "Captain," derived from the parties he gave aboard a small yacht harbored in the bay waters that coasted the state capital. On many a morning, officials could not remember the night before, but they were certain they had a good time. In return, the "Captain" was favored at contract awards time.

Herman's son came into the business immediately after high school. He loved his father and imitated his lifestyle. Bill began drinking in his teens. Herman was proud of his son and often remarked, "That boy will go somewhere. He can really hold his liquor." By the time he got out of school, young Bill Moser was an alcoholic.

At twenty Bill married Marge, who loved the party atmosphere of the Moser family. She understood Bill's ill-temper after an especially heavy night of drinking and catered to him. Her own father was an alcoholic, but "lovable." Bill and Marge had four sons and a daughter.

Substance Abuse

Two of Bill's children chose not to go into the family business. The daughter, Angie, went to college for several years but was eventually dismissed because of her "good time" attitude, which put partying before schoolwork. The youngest son, Eddie, loved sports and became a star football player. He was drafted by a professional football team, which overlooked his substance abuse problems in an atmosphere of injury-related drug use.

The other three sons—Johnny, Pat, and Sam—went into the family business and continued the "booze and build" tradition of the Moser family. To it they added two new substances, cocaine and marijuana, which were popular and easy to come by for people with money and a good time on their minds. At this point, the Moser family was supporting seven people with serious substance abuse problems, and the profits began to reflect it.

Johnny, Pat, and Sam Moser were inseparable. They drank together every night after work and their family lives were intermeshed. They understood each other's problems and they also realized that the company supported their lifestyles. When Pat, who headed scheduling, began to make major, costly mistakes, Johnny and Sam began to worry. Then they discovered Pat had a drug problem that siphoned off more than they "allowed" for drug and alcohol use. (They actually maintained an envelope of cash for purchasing alcohol and illegal substances.)

One day Johnny was almost killed in a job-related accident. He was hospitalized for several months, which forcibly dried him out. His treatment was complicated by his long-standing use of alcohol, and in the end he partially lost the use of one hand damaged in the accident. Johnny had a long time to think in the hospital and resolved to stop drinking. He was the eldest. He had always set the pace. He was the one his brothers looked up to. His decision to stop led Pat and Sam to do the same.

The one thing that kept the brothers on their new path was

the support they gave each other. None wanted to see the other two fail. Within the company they adopted a slogan, "If you're wired, you're fired." Alcohol or drug use on the job meant immediate dismissal. A number of employees were terminated during the first year of the policy because the problem had filtered down into all layers of the company. Since the brothers all went into treatment for their problems, they encouraged employees to do the same. They even paid for the treatment, and kept a valued person on full pay during a drying-out process.

The Moser family had always done things in a big way. They attacked a problem and expected to win. The road to recovery from long-term substance abuse was difficult and required professional counseling. But they made it. Several years later, the Moser business was not only clean of abusive substances but headed toward its highest profits ever. The brothers also sought outside advice to help them professionalize their management. They made the transition with few snags and began to replace their macho reputation with one of excellence at the best price.

Eddie, the athlete, and Angie, the sister, had a harder time. Alcohol complicated Angie's first pregnancy, and she lost the child. Eddie's athletic career suffered because of his off-season bouts of brawling and drug use. He continued on this path, despite his brothers' urgings, because his "world" supported substance abuse. Only after their grandfather's death from alcohol-related disorders and diabetes did Angie and Eddie attempt to do something about their problems.

As the Mosers learned, it is difficult to determine how much of a good thing is too much. A rule of thumb is: "Can I get through the day without it? And tomorrow? And the day after?" If the answer is no, the problem is serious. If the answer is "Yes, but I don't want to," ask yourself why. The problem may be greater than you think. Today the onus of *getting* help is being replaced by that of *refusing* to get help. Families need to support those who seek to untangle themselves from addictive behavior. A new set of family messages needs to be constructed.

In the end, a family in business needs to ask itself if what it has built is in danger of being destroyed by substance abuse. If the answer is "yes," then alcohol and drugs are that family's biggest competitor for profits and longevity.

9

The Whos and Hows of Succession

Why is it that choosing a family member to head a business can lead its other members to drastic acts—not only to alcoholism but also to fratricide, patricide, and suicide? Every emotion imaginable transpires when the family's business successor is announced. The popularity of *Dallas, Dynasty,* and other "empire series" on TV attests to the universality of the emotions involved.

Are there ways to avoid all the unpleasantries surrounding this issue? Can there be orderly succession in a family business? Is it possible for all family members to win *without* each having the top job? How the succession issue is handled determines the future health of the family business and its members.

The Importance of Planning

The illness or death of a founder is not the proper time to begin discussion of this delicate subject. Some families are capable of pulling the pieces together through the mourning period and continuing in business. But they need not struggle in a situation where advanced planning could have smoothed the way. Other families do not have the skills or knowledge to keep the enterprise functioning—because the founder never addressed the succession problem. It was certainly one of the most important issues of his business career, and he neglected it. The problem may have been that the founder never put management of his enterprise on a professional business footing. Correcting this situation is the top priority of the successor.

Or the problem may have been the founder's inability to let go of the enterprise, for reasons previously discussed. Regardless of training, grooming, and planning, no successor can succeed if the predecessor refuses to phase out. "I know I should let go, but what will I do?" is the common complaint. The answer is to *plan ahead* for the continued profits of the enterprise. The consequences of not letting go can be damaging to the successor and destructive to the business itself.

Consider the business owner who refuses to relinquish control, is unwilling to delegate responsibility, and withholds essential information from key members within the business. Suddenly, he dies and his bereaved family is left without the tools needed to carry on the enterprise. Since the business is valuable primarily as an ongoing entity that produces revenue for its owners, a liquidation or short-notice sale robs them of future profits. More than one family has discovered, when selling a business under duress, that its value is less than they had anticipated.

Then there is the predecessor who has second thoughts and comes back to "meddle" in the business. Such a psychological disruption is unhealthy for the entire family. The process is helped greatly when the retiring founder has activities, hobbies, or interests outside the business that he wants to pursue. He decides life is worth living outside the enterprise.

Involvement in those outside interests must begin well before the time to let go.

In other cases, the entrepreneur may want time off from the business but refuse to allow anyone else to take full control. Charlie Lake did this initially with his son-in-law, Andrew. Charlie kept his title and position as president so he could return occasionally to "shape things up." It took him a long time to let go and he did so only when he became convinced that the business could go on without him. At the same time, he became interested in restoring antique airplanes and flying them cross-country. The business took too much time away from his new "love," and he decided to install Andrew once and for all in the command seat, but without the authority the position commanded. Until Charlie was willing to accept his son-in-law's entrepreneurial talents, Andrew's choices were limited and the growth of the business was stifled.

"Where Is the Business Going?"

The simplest way to plan for succession is to ask two questions: "Where is the business going?" and "Who in the family—if anyone—has the skills and leadership abilities needed to get it there?" These questions are a nonthreatening way for the family to confront the complicated issues of succession. When nonfamily members currently hold responsible positions in management, they should be included in the successor selection process. Not only will they have valuable insights; they may also have the skills necessary to develop the next phase of the business.

Every day, business leaders make predictions about the future. They speculate on whether the market will rise or fall, on which products should be produced for greatest revenues, on what the whims of the consumer will be. One of the peculiar "genius" traits of the entrepreneur is his ability to recognize trends in the consumer market that can lead to greater profits. It is not unlikely that one or more of the possible successors has this ability. If not, it is doubly important for the family to chart a course for the business while the entrepreneur is still at the helm. His guidelines will be invaluable to future expansion decisions and to the ultimate continued success of the business.

Asking where the business is going introduces the entrepreneur to the idea that the business must be *professionalized*. This means that the successor must have definite skills. With this in mind, the family can begin to chart a profile of those skills. The business must move from an entrepreneurial style to a highly refined professional management. These two styles are dramatically different. The net effect of asking the opening question is to depersonalize the succession decision and make it more objective.

When succession is approached in this way, and all family members and unrelated potential successors are included in the development of a viable solution, the entrepreneur is saved the agonizing decision of choosing among children. The focus becomes the business and its future rather than a coronation of the favored one. On the other hand, when the decision is left solely to the founder/entrepreneur, the rest of the family will believe he has designated his favorite person. This may or may not be so. The objective process simply eliminates the possibility that an older child will be selected purely because of birth order and regardless of interest or ability.

The entrepreneur must stick to the family decision and not cut a private deal with another family member—for example, by willing that member his share of the company. If this occurs, the controlling interest will be held by a person who does not fit the profile of a successor. The conflicts that can occur in such a situation are too numerous to mention here. The successor must be in a position of authority for the plan to work.

The Whos and Hows of Succession

When a succession program is designed well in advance of the entrepreneur's retirement, there is time to train a successor in the needed skills. This training does not necessarily mean a college education. In some cases, a college degree program may be too time-consuming, and the degree itself will not guarantee success. The best route is to tailor a program to the specific individual.

One essential in any training program is for the entrepreneur to brief the successor about phases of the business. This is an ongoing process to the day he steps down. If for some reason the entrepreneur is not available, and the program needs to move quickly, experts in various fields can be engaged to teach the successor needed skills. These experts may be found in the local community or in major business centers. Family dynasties like the Kennedys and the Rockefellers are noted for their "brain trusts"—for hiring outside professionals who keep family members informed of state-of-the-art thinking in a variety of fields. There are also specialized training programs in leadership and communication. For example, at The Center for Creative Leadership* this type of instruction is available. The center provides practical, research-based tools and offers training programs developed from its studies of effective management techniques.

Another time-honored method of training a family member is mentoring. The ideal mentor is someone in the same business field as the potential successor and ten to fifteen years older. A larger age span between the mentor and his charge will bring the relationship into a parental framework; a small age span will make it more of a peer experience. The job of the mentor is to share experiences with the younger person and guide him through the brambles of the business. Generally, the relationship lasts until the young person is thirty to thirty-five.

*The Center for Creative Leadership is located at 5000 Laurinda Drive, P.O. Box P-1, Greensboro, North Carolina 27402; the phone number is 919-288-7210.

By that time, the apprentice should know much of what the mentor has to teach and be ready to strike out on his own. Drifting apart from the mentor at this point is a normal occurrence.

Parents can act as mentors, but the relationship is potentially more difficult. If the parent identifies too much with being a mentor, he will be hurt in the normal separation process and may become resentful. The resentment of one typical father-mentor was evident when he told his son, who was in the drifting phase, "After all I've done for you—I taught you everything I know—now you don't even ask my opinion." The father has reached the stage where he wants acknowledgment and credit while the son or daughter is ready to move on, take more responsibility, and perhaps be on his or her own. Recognition of these diverse, predictable developmental steps will make it easier to accept the process of drifting apart.

Grooming Children for Succession

Grooming children for entry into the family business can begin at an early age. The attitudes of children toward the business will be formed by their parents' discussion of the business at home. When parents are positive about the challenges and demands of their work, the children will adopt a similar viewpoint.

Involving children in a phase of the enterprise that is appropriate for their age is an added benefit. The parent or an employee can instruct the child in a necessary skill. Children who have "fun" in the family business grow up with good attitudes toward it and have a sense of pride in belonging to their family. Too many families think that the only place to start a child is at the business end of a broom on the loading dock. Not so.

Children who learn the value of work early in life will

make the greatest contributions to the success of their business later on. No matter how much money a family has at its disposal, the child who learns how to make legitimate and constructive contributions to his life will have a sense of self-worth and a postive attitude toward family and society. This will be a confidant and ultimately successful child.

On January 20, 1985, *The Washington Post Magazine* carried an article about local children who were involved in their own businesses.[1] The oldest of these entrepreneurial kids was eighteen. John Shorb opened a lawn service business that grossed $60,000 in the six months after he graduated from high school. He began his business in the fifth grade by cutting lawns. Now he does his own books and billings and has two full-time employees. He foresees his company becoming a major horticultural center in Washington. The biggest headache for John is his taxes. His reaction to his 25 to 30 percent bracket is the same as that of any adult.

David Stern was given a computer by his parents in the sixth grade. In turn, he taught his family about computers. His mother, Rosalind, went on to work on an M.A. in computer education and his father began to learn word processing. The family worked together and encouraged one another. By the end of the eighth grade, David was earning more than $100 a week teaching computer applications and programming to other schoolchildren. Now in the tenth grade, he is the president of Design Soft, a software and computer education consulting program. He and his mother are at work on educational programs which they hope to publish.

Both John and David learned about work, its joys, and its problems. Both were encouraged by their families. In David's case, he involved his entire family in computing, so the family has a business outside the parents' professional careers. Children who grow up in family businesses may not have this entrepreneurial opportunity because the business is already on track and in place. But they need the same type of experience

117

as these two young men and the same encouraging, participatory attitude on the part of the parents.

Building a Decision-Making Unit

There is yet another reason for involving potential successors early on. The entire family will learn to work together as a decision-making unit before a crisis occurs. There are countless stories of heirs to family fortunes or businesses who cannot agree on anything, who simply end up "pulling and tugging" at each other like siblings or cousins at a family picnic. They argue over estates and how they are to be used, over the gifting of art treasures or stock or furniture. In most cases, they hire lawyers to do the "pulling and tugging" for them. This results in a high expense in lawyers' fees and in bad feelings in general. To avoid acting in selfish, immature ways when it comes to the family business, children *and* adults must start early to work together and develop healthy ways to solve problems. For example, the broadcasting and publishing empire of the Bingham family of Louisville, Kentucky was sold because the successors never learned to work together.

As previously mentioned, successor generations can fail or falter because they lack knowledge in financial matters. It is imperative for parents to include children in discussions of the family and business finances. These matters can be tailored to the age of the child, but they must take place. As children grow older, they can be exposed to more complicated financial matters and encouraged to manage their own funds. Children enjoy money management because it gives them a sense of control over their lives. For example, a child might be given a sum of money for specific expenses over a set period of time. The sum must be adequate to cover the amount the child will need with some left over. The time span must be long enough for a sense of real management to occur. The child can then decide how and when to spend the money.

One family gives its children a quarterly sum for clothing and spending money. The children can spend as little or as much of the money as they desire, but if the money is spent before the allotted time, no more is forthcoming. In another family, the children are given an annual allowance for specific expenses. If they go over this amount, they may borrow on the following year's money, but one time only. The sum borrowed is deducted from the next year's allowance.

Allowing children to handle money early on encourages good decision making. Sometimes, of course, the learning takes place through hindsight. One young man received his clothing allowance for a school quarter. He immediately spent more than half of it on a single pair of pants. Several weeks later, when he needed other clothes, he said to his father, "You know, Dad, I spent too much on those pants. I should have used the money for at least two pairs!" For this learning procedure to be worthwhile, the child must receive enough money to manage. Children who are nickel-and-dimed will never learn to manage their resources properly.

Financial discussions at home have another value. Children need to be conscious of the source of the money that maintains their lifestyle. Full disclosure of finances promotes responsible money management as a habit in young and older children alike. Thus trained, children will not be easy prey to the indulgent lifestyles that destroy the potential of many children of wealth.

Orderly Succession

A smooth transition in a family business requires that a successor be chosen long before the founder leaves. The successor must be trained in skill-deficient areas in order to make the transition to the top spot. At this time, the family should prepare a *written* contract that clearly defines responsibilities during the transition. Such a contract would be expected in an outside company; the family-controlled enterprise is no different. It is another way of professionalizing the business.

A periodic review of performance during the transition is essential. This can be done by an outside adviser—for example, a leader from a local business school or a responsible businessperson who runs a well-managed business. Regularly scheduled performance reviews give the successor the opportunity to receive positive and negative feedback on his progress. It also allows him to fine-tune his role in keeping with the company's objectives. Of no less importance is the fact that the successor can develop confidence. Finally, putting performance evaluation on a sound business basis reduces the likelihood that interpersonal, family-related issues will cloud professional judgment. All results in business are achieved through others. Therefore, *the successor has to be a good "psychologist."* Excellent people skills are essential for building a positive atmosphere within the company. Someone who lacks these skills, regardless of any other qualifications, can obtain only short-term results. By the same token, the skilled "people" person must have the other qualifications for management, especially in the financial area. *In fact, the more the business grows, the more skillful the management must become in financial matters.*

The most frequent problem in family-controlled business is the failure of the retiring founder to train the successor in the financial aspects of the business. Lack of business skills, especially in finances, holds many potential successors back. Here again, women are the biggest losers. Many women have the people skills, enthusiasm, drive, and desire to enter the business world. But they have not acquired money management expertise. A well-rounded training program can correct this deficiency. The important issue here is to consider not only those who have the skills at present but those who could easily develop them.

Prudent decisions in a growing business often become a

matter of sound cash management of cash reserves. It is the wise owner who early on openly discusses all the money aspects of the enterprise with his family as well as with any other appropriate members of the successor group. This matter can be complicated by the ego of an entrepreneur who may be reluctant to share such details with anyone. However, the issue must be addressed.

Since keeping the business viable and thriving is the objective, the *successor's view of the company* is important because of its impact on the rest of the enterprise. He must be prepared to move confidently into the future. To maintain the business at its current level is equivalent to going backward. During the first stages of his tenure, the successor has to gather and assess data with the idea always in mind of vigorously pursuing the next level of business aspiration. The successor, along with all other key talent available, must develop a new "dream" of what the business can become.

Successors Must Be Their Own People

Businesses transferred between generations are often so heavily influenced by the personality of the founder or predecessor that the new leader is restricted in the operation. It is not easy to live in the shadow of a powerful leader. The successor needs to establish his own support system to maintain proper perspective on the complicated circumstances of a family business.

In 1976, a number of young men in Boston who were employed by their fathers formed a group called SOBs—sons of bosses. They banded together as a support system and felt free to lament their plight at having to work for a powerful parent. As they matured, they expanded their base and "colonized" other organizations around the United States. Some of the new members objected to the name SOBs because it emphasized the hostility, anger, and resentment they felt toward

121

their fathers. The title started as a joke, but every joke has an element of truth that makes it serious.

Entry into the family business must be by choice and not coercion. Not all possible successors want the job. An entrepreneur may expect his oldest son to enter the business. This is fine if the son wants to do so and has the qualifications. However, if he shows signs of reluctance, he must not be bribed or pressured by financial rewards inappropriate to his skills or to the position. On the other hand, he should not expect to share equally in the profits with those who do enter the business. Family members who are actively involved in daily operations should be compensated for their increased responsibility.

A shared last name is not reason enough for a person to be in the family business, much less to be a successor and be paid more than "fair market value for the job." A legitimate job must exist for the family member, and he must have the skills to do it. When an unqualified family member is simply installed in a job, employees and other family members will regard it as a case of birthright. The resulting bitterness and resentment will lead the appointed family member to lose confidence and self-respect. Whatever talent that person may have will be overlooked or underrated as he struggles to find his "niche" in the company—a struggle that could have been avoided by matching the skills to the job.

Enter *with* Portfolio

A family member who enters the business *with portfolio* has the best chance of success. This portfolio is one of experience and should contain some or all of the following:

1. Three to five years of employment in a job or jobs that have depended on competence, skill, and sustained

performance, rather than on family-based relationships. At least one of those jobs should have lasted two years or more and included promotion. (Two years in a job is ample opportunity to demonstrate competence and earn promotion.)

2. Experience in directing the activities of others.
3. Recognition for demonstrated competence in the job.
4. Evidence of ability to manage relationships, both with peers and with superiors.
5. Evidence of ability and willingness to take initiative on the job.
6. Evidence of having been a valued employee with legitimate contributions to make.

At least two things are gained by such out-of-family training. The person learns the basics of business in an atmosphere where mistakes are considered part of the learning process and are not tied to past errors within the family. Next, the person has the opportunity to test his fundamental ideas about himself and gain feedback from people who can view him objectively. He is not coddled, nor is his behavior rationalized because of his family connections. In short, he rises or falls on his own skills, talent, and drive. He builds a professional image of himself. Success in an outside business gives him perspective and confidence that are hard to gain within the family enterprise, where it is difficult not to be viewed as "special" in some sense.

An excellent example of out-of-family training is the Men's Apparel Forum, a national association of top-of-the-line men's clothing and furnishings stores. The group members train each other's successors from noncompetitive markets or different geographical areas. It has found that exchanging successors to teach them the basics of the clothing business is very valuable and fosters a sense of cooperation throughout their industry. Two scrap-iron dealers, one in New Jersey and one in Brussels, exchanged sons over a period of two years. During this time, each son was taken through preplanned training procedures and taught the business.

Such arrangements can range from very loosely structured to highly formalized contracts with specific outlines for the number of months to be spent and the amount of responsibility to be handled. Once again, the learning process must be designed to fit the needs of the people involved.

In this chapter the importance of succession has been emphasized, and the various problems that can arise if succession is not planned for by the family have been enumerated. In the next chapter common models for succession will be outlined, thus rounding out my discussion of an area that cannot be ignored if a family business is to prosper and flourish.

10

Succession Plans

Models for succession are limited only by the number of families in business and their particular circumstances. The models described in this chapter show the most common successor situations and how they can be handled. Underlying all of them is the critical need, examined in the last chapter, for selecting and grooming the successor generation. In order for all family members to be in a win-win position—to feel they have benefited by the succession—a well-thought-out plan is essential. When succession is left to the whims of fate, the family's empire begins to crumble under waves of emotion. A family business deserves more than that.

Succession by a Single Heir

By far the least complicated successor model is that of the single heir who wants to join the family business, is expected to, and is groomed by the parents to do so. Traditionally, this is the oldest son. On his own or with encouragement from his father, the son acquires the skills and education needed to move the business forward. The father is pleased with his son's progress and stays on in a limited, advisory role after the son assumes the business reins.

Unfortunately, this ideal scenario rarely happens. The picture gets complicated in many ways. Often, as we have seen, the entrepreneur simply will not let go. Another problem arises when the logical successor is a daughter. Because of her gender, her parents may have overlooked her desire and talent, or they may have a prejudice about women in business. On her part, she may not want to assume a role in the family business regardless of her education, skills, and ability.

Henrietta Howland Robinson Green (1834–1916), "the witch of Wall Street," exemplifies this problem. Hetty was a most reluctant heir. Her older brother died in infancy, and against her wishes her father insisted *she* learn to manage the money she inherited from the family's whaling and trade business. A cool, efficient, and shrewd businessman, her father supervised her financial training, which started before she was twelve. Hetty's personal development was by the pressure of having to succeed in "a man's world" during an era when women were groomed for dependent roles. However, she learned her lessons well and increased her inheritance from $1,000,000 to $100,000,000.

In turn, Hetty groomed her oldest son for management of her vast holdings. She allowed him to gain experience outside her companies and to develop his own interests. In addition, he was educated as a lawyer. In later life, when her son was installed as president of her numerous enterprises, Hetty turned back to those things she had missed as a young girl. Thought to be senile and "crazy," she went barefoot in the streets. Hetty's money had finally given her the opportunity to have the childhood she had missed.

Succession by Multiple Heirs

It is common for a family to have more than one member who expects to, hopes to, or does inherit the business. This situation can cause a variety of difficulties that disrupt the smooth flow of business as well as family unity. The following model for multiple succession shows how potentially disastrous family business situations can be handled effectively. The model works especially well with a small group of heirs who are not yet involved in the family business. They may be completing their educations or serving apprenticeships in other businesses.

In this model, the heirs are taught how to handle a business as a group and protect the money that accrues to them. None of them may choose to go into the family business, but they will know enough about it to make responsible decisions if the business is turned over to them. They learn to cooperate in a professional way as they manage their legacy.

A written plan gives them guidelines for behaviors and decisions. The plan includes forming a new corporation capitalized by the group of successors. This corporation or partnership made up of siblings then elects officers with defined responsibilities. This approach provides the heirs with an opportunity to experience working together in financial matters. The responsibility of each person ranges from managing the cash and making investments to procedures for disbursing money. Siblings learn what constitutes a proper decision. Procedures for settling differences are outlined in the written plan.

This type of training gives designated successors the opportunity to become competent, prudent, and responsible managers who can negotiate effectively among themselves rather than use "hired guns" to do it for them. Most important, the successors gain experience as a unit focused on business matters.

127

Family Business, Risky Business

There is no limit to the number of legal arrangements that can be worked out when multiple heirs are involved. The heirs need not be siblings, but may simply be related by bloodlines or marriage. In one business, four cousins each managed a different division. Each was capable and successful in his own way. But when it came to overall business planning or sticky financial planning, they engaged an outside business consultant to keep them on target. If one of the four cousins disagreed with a decision, he could call for review by an outside arbitrator. The heirs agreed, in advance, to be bound by the arbitrator's decision. However, if one of the four called for arbitration three times in five years and was decided against by the arbitrator each time, he was required to sell his interest to the other three members at a price arrived at by a predetermined formula. This arrangement kept any one heir from entrenching his position until the company was in jeopardy and the other heirs relented. It forced each to take a reasoned position that would stand the review of an outsider. Also, each heir knew in advance the full consequences of being unwilling to work out a compromise. As a result, petty arguments were reduced and the professionalism of the management was enhanced.

A note of caution here. The arbitrator in such a case must be completely free of any profit from the decision he makes. Thus, company lawyers and accountants are not usually wise choices. Moreover, the arbitrator must be a professional who is well schooled in business matters and understands the intricacies of the issue at hand. The family described above specified that a member of the American Arbitration Association be used, should an arbitrator be needed.

Multiple-heir successions often work surprisingly well. The Bass brothers, the four nephews of Texas oil billionaire Sid Richardson, have continued to build a business dynasty on their uncle's oil fortune.[1] Ranging in age from forty-two to twenty-eight, they are sophisticated, ambitious, and well-trained businessmen who have a social conscience. Each works hard to ensure the continued success of the family's far-reaching financial enterprises. Without their professional attitude toward management and willingness to call in expert advice, this family empire could easily have crumbled under incredible business strife. On the contrary, the Bass's are considered the modern-day heirs to the Morgan and Rockefeller family business tradition.

The Inactive Owner

As a general principle, countless problems can be avoided if family members who do not intend to be active in the business are not left stock in it. The interests of inactive members are antithetical to those of active family members. Simply stated, *inactive owners usually want cash.*

The active, operating members of the business have intimate knowledge of its plans and financial needs. These include the need for capital improvements, expansion, and maintaining marketing position. To avoid conflicts between active and inactive members, it is better for the inactive members to be willed assets other than corporate stock. If stock is willed, restrictive clauses should be included so that it may not be sold outside the family or, at the very least, so that the business retains the right of first refusal in any sale.

Such an arrangement should also include a schedule and formula for redemption of the stock over a specific time period. The formula should be tied to ratios on the corporate balance sheet so that sales of stock by inactive family members will not jeopardize the financial position of the company. In no case should payment be *on demand.* Failure to include these conditions nearly forced a business with $12 million in sales into bankruptcy when a family member demanded payment.

Sometimes the cleanest way to maintain the business is for the successor to buy it outright. In such a case, the predecessor must have complete confidence in the ability of the successor. After all, it is the successful business that will generate revenues that provide money for the buyout.

Proper contracts must be drawn that clearly define the expectations of all parties. Each party needs to know what the other will do and how it will be done. An excellent example is the Dillon brothers, who owned a business together. George had twins who were active in the business; Jim had one son who was also active. George wanted his brother to gift his share in such a way that the three heirs would receive equal ownership. This meant that Jim would be giving a portion of his equity to his nephews. He resisted. In addition, he decided he did not want his son in business with the twin nephews. Then, one of George's twin sons decided he did not want to be in a position where he would be influenced by his brother and his cousin.

The solution was for each father to gift one share to each son, making the twins and their cousin equal owners. Then the three cousins entered into an arrangement to purchase the remaining shares held by their fathers. The details of the purchase agreement were precise in terms of what was to be paid, how, and when. The three cousins also agreed that if any one of them felt a decision was being forced on him, or was not in the best interests of the company, an outside arbitrator would be brought in to resolve the case. The three agreed to be bound by the decision of the arbitrator—a member of the American Arbitration Association. The fact that a written arrangement existed to resolve such difficulties helped to keep them from occurring.

The Widow as Successor

The founder's wife is very often overlooked as a successor. Yet her talents and interest in the business may be equal to or greater than those of the sons, daughters, sisters, brothers, and cousins who are seen as possible successors. There are many examples of women succeeding to their husbands' place and taking the company to new heights of profit.

However, if the woman has had no business training or has been excluded from financial decisions, she may find the problems of the business too difficult. She has the usual options of selling the business or turning it over to a favored child. If neither of these options appeals to her, she can bring in professional management, though this could change the character of the company and might jeopardize her best interests. Consequently, if the wife is the selected heir, she must be made aware of her increased responsibility and the operation of the business before a change forces her to inappropriate decisions.

Unrelated Successors

Successors may not be found within the family. There may be no children, or the children may lack interest or have other career ambitions. In this case, the family should look within the company ranks for someone who has the necessary skills to succeed to the top position. If such a person cannot be found, the only choice is to look to outside management.

The criteria for choosing an unrelated successor include skills, experience, and an ability to carry on the family tradition, if that is desired. Many companies have a well-developed social image linked to their product as well. Others use business funds for political or artistic ends. The incoming professional must be aware of the ramifications of these interests, which could put restraints on his management style or decisions. These areas should be clearly spelled out because they will ultimately affect his career as well. This is especially important if large portions of the profits are allotted to charitable or political ends. Professional management will find it difficult to operate in a business climate where decisions can be arbitrarily reversed because of the family's personal agenda. All profits will be "at risk."

Succeeding at Succession: The Harwoods' Happy Ending

The succession program for the Harwood family was phased in over a three-year period with benchmarks to measure the success of each phase. All family members worked hard to implement it. Louis, Sr. went away for a much needed rest. Charles agreed to stay with the firm until Elaine could dispose of her company, which she immediately put up for sale. Within six months, she had negotiated the contract and moved back to her home town. In the meantime, she met regularly with Charles and Lou to learn about their experience in the business.

The two-month rest was instrumental in controlling Louis, Sr.'s blood pressure and in giving him time to reflect on his decision. When he explored the possibilities, he finally admitted to himself that he wanted new challenges. He came back from his leave with a plan for taking Elaine rapidly through the instructional phase of the business. As Louis continued to recognize her entrepreneurial qualities, he also understood that Elaine would become the business peer in whose hands he could safely entrust his life's efforts. She totally appreciated the skill and determination he had expended to make the company successful.

As they began working together, Louis introduced Elaine to his clients and the Harwood financial sources. To his surprise, they accepted her success in her business without mentioning the fact that she was a woman. In fact, Louis was complimented for having "the guts to put the right person in the job." Elaine's knowledge of finance and ways to capitalize the expansion wiped away any lingering doubt Louis had about her ability to handle a manufacturing company.

Elaine's permanent move back to her home town and Charles's departure from the company ended the first phase of the transition. In the next phase, Louis, Sr. limited his participation, gradually letting go of operational responsibility and serving only as a consultant. He realized he had grown tired of certain phases of the business. Basically, he no longer wanted to be "tied down" to the responsibilities of an expanding corporation. Other ideas—ones he had not been able to entertain for years—were beginning to interest him more.

During the second phase, Bill Archer began a slow transfer of power to Louis, Jr. Lou responded enthusiastically, buoyed by Elaine's encouragement to use his skills. The plans he developed for the plant expansion made it unnecessary for the family to call in an outside engineer. Louis, Sr. began to view his son's ability in a different light. They reduced costs and improved production.

Charles's problems took time. He entered a substance abuse program shortly after learning of his complex medical condition. His initial relief to find his family supportive of his desire to get out of the business was tempered by a gradual recognition that he had nothing else to do. After Phase One was in place, Charles suffered a severe depression, including a suicide attempt that required further hospitalization. Regular psychotherapy was added to his alcohol abuse program.

Given the length of Charles's depression and its underlying causes, he made surprising progress. Within three years, Charles had opened an art gallery in the same city in which Elaine had established her first business. She introduced him to friends and former clients. This entree, combined with his knowledge of business principles, brought him rapid success. Charles indulged his love for the theater by promoting a local acting company and sometimes doing onstage roles himself. The praise he drew from critics and friends added to his confidence in his new direction in life.

In addition, Charles remained a consultant to the family

business and a member of its board. For the first time, he enjoyed the interaction with his sister and brother. At first, his father had felt betrayed to learn of Charles's obvious dislike for the business. Then he became confused and angered by the suicide attempt. But the long and close relationship the two had shared prompted Louis to make the extra effort to understand Charles's emotional problems. Louis offered him every support in his efforts to conquer his difficulties. To this day, Louis still calls Charles to talk about "details." The difference is his son feels free to end the conversation or to supply his own "endless details." Along the way, Charles has learned to express his feelings and Louis has learned to listen. This exemplifies Charles's increased level of differentiation.

As Louis, Sr. phased himself out of the business, he and Lillian traveled widely. After each trip, he came back with new insights into the forces that guide national and international economics. Elaine and Lillian encouraged him to lecture to interested groups on what he had learned. He did so and enjoyed himself immensely. He began to receive requests for transcripts of his lectures, which led to his first book, *A Nation's Business—A Nation's Pride.* The book enjoyed a considerable trade sale and was used as a supplementary text in college business and economics courses.

As for Lillian, she fulfilled her life-long ambition to see most of the world's great public art collections and a few of the private ones. More important to her was the time she had with her husband and the new camaraderie the family enjoyed.

Establishing a succession plan did not close the Harwood case. The most difficult thing for the family was to temper its inclination to move ahead too quickly. The nature of the manufacturing business, the time necessary to relocate Elaine, and the urgency Charles felt to be totally out from under threatened on several occasions to undermine what they had accomplished. As consultant, it was my responsibility to keep them on target.

Succession Plans

The Harwood successor story has a happy ending. It is not so for so many families who fail to perceive the real issues facing them. It took a major health problem and the possible loss of the family enterprise before the Harwoods would confront their problems. Then it took hard work and good faith on the part of each family member to devise and accept solutions that would keep the family and the business intact. Their willingness to learn new techniques for conducting interpersonal relationships and implementing changes paid off as a prosperous era opened for Harwood E&C.

This success can be repeated by any real family in business that steps back from undermining itself to admit: "We need help." Information on how a family in business should proceed once it has reached this step can be found in the Appendix.

11

Sound Business Practice

The purpose of any business is to generate profits for its owners. More than one family has found itself in trouble because it lost sight of this simple fact. Business owners who say, "This is mine and I will do with it what I please," are forgetting their responsibilities. Whether there are two hundred, two thousand, or twenty thousand employees, the owner has an obligation to operate the business in the most professional manner possible. Employees are expected to perform at the peak of their capabilities, and they, in turn, have the right to expect the business to operate in a manner that ensures continuity and stability. Users of the product or service have a right to expect the same.

This means that the family in business must understand sound business practice and how it is affected by family dynamics. It is not my purpose here to define all that constitutes sound business practice. Many excellent works on the topic are listed at the end of this book. What is important here is to determine if a company is operating in as professional a manner as possible and, if not, what can be done about it.

The "Healthy Business" Test

In the course of my work with family-owned businesses, I found it necessary to devise a method to make a quick assessment of the health and soundness of the company. This assessment focuses on the relationships within the business. It is a simple method of pinpointing trouble areas. Grounded in sound management theory, it offers a profile of how the people within a business view it and of their attitudes concerning the company's choice of procedures and methods. Bear in mind, it is always a *subjective* assessment. There are those who advocate objective assessment of the business climate. My experience suggests that objective assessment means little to the parties in the middle of the business environment. If a family member believes conditions are a certain way, no "objective" assessment will change that view.

The Healthy Business Test, shown in Figure 7, aids family members in taking another, fresher look at the business. Family members given the form must receive the following instructions before they fill it out:

1. There are *no* right answers.
2. If a statement is confusing, do not be concerned, but complete it according to your best understanding.
3. Explain why you checked what you did on the 1 to 9 continuum (1 is the lowest point, 9 is the highest).

After all parties have completed the form, a composite is made of their responses. On the composite no record is kept of the sources of the checks or comments. The composite is

138

presented to all parties, who then discuss the results. Assume, for example, that four people checked the "Goals" continuum at 3, 4, 5, and 7. This suggests that three of them are much less satisfied with the status quo than the fourth. The next step is to clarify their positions and make a plan to address their concerns. The real value is in the discussion and clarification that take place.

When studying the six areas on the Healthy Business Test, it is useful to think of the prevailing patterns in a family as they relate to these six functions. The closer family patterns are to the higher end of the scale, the closer the family is to establishing sound business practice and a healthy business climate. If the operating manner of the family is not in sync with sound business practice as indicated by the lower end of the scale, it is quite likely that function is or will become a problem area for the family enterprise. Recognizing and understanding the connection between the six areas of sound business practice and family functioning is the heart of the integrated view of family business.

The Importance of Goals

A more thorough understanding of this issue can be gained from an examination of what *goals* mean to the success of a business.

In 1974 David Campbell, a prominent psychologist, wrote *If You Don't Know Where You're Going, You'll Probably End Up Somewhere Else.*[1] The catchy title describes exactly what happens to people and businesses when they are without goals. In a healthy business, goals are carefully articulated in writing. For example: "We are a market-driven manufacturer of packaged cereal products until 1990." This deceptively simple statement contains goals for the present and implies those for the future. Throughout the total business—among its subparts and

Figure 7.   How healthy is your business?

1. <u>GOALS</u>

The total business, subparts, and individuals manage their work against goals and plan for achievement of these goals. Goals are written and shared by all owners.

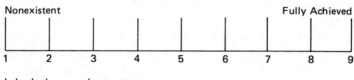

Nonexistent ... Fully Achieved

I checked _____ because:

2. <u>DECISION MAKING</u>

Decisions are made by and near the sources of information, regardless of where these sources are located on the organization chart. In fact, a decision is made at the lowest level possible for that decision.

Nonexistent ... Fully Achieved

I checked _____ because:

3. <u>COMMUNICATION</u>

Communication laterally and vertically is relatively undistorted. Clear messages are given and received. There are no secrets.

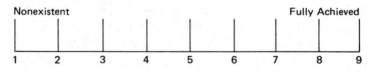

Nonexistent ... Fully Achieved

I checked _____ because:

Sound Business Practice

4. WIN-WIN BEHAVIOR

There is a maximum amount of win-win behavior and a minimum amount of inappropriate win-lose behavior between individuals and groups. The focus is on mutually beneficial outcomes for parties to the transaction. The norm is for all to <u>feel</u> good about themselves, their work, and each other.

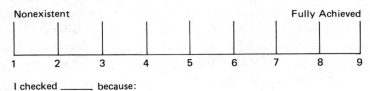

Nonexistent   Fully Achieved

1   2   3   4   5   6   7   8   9

I checked _____ because:

5. CONFLICT MANAGEMENT

There is high "conflict" (clash of ideas) about tasks and projects and relatively little energy spent in clashing over interpersonal difficulties because they have been generally worked through and resolved.

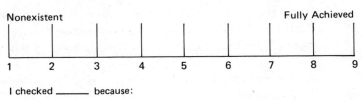

Nonexistent   Fully Achieved

1   2   3   4   5   6   7   8   9

I checked _____ because:

6. LEARNING FROM EXPERIENCE

People are allowed to learn from experience. Mistakes are a normal part of learning. Individuals are neither restricted nor held back in their opportunity to assume responsibility. When mistakes do occur, they are openly analyzed with appropriate strategies made to avoid repeating them.

Nonexistent   Fully Achieved

1   2   3   4   5   6   7   8   9

I checked _____ because:

individuals—the work is managed toward these goals and thus the company plans for its achievement.

In my work with family business owners, I ask the question: "Do you have goals or business plans in which the specifics are described in writing?" Usually fewer than 10 percent have such a document. The value of agreed-upon goals should be obvious. They focus the energy of all people on specific objectives. Also, written goals can be referenced. Family members can measure their success by comparing their actual performance with the written objectives.

One business owner told me his objective was to make profits. When I asked for a breakdown of the source of the profits, the owner could not provide an adequate answer. He had not thought it through sufficiently to determine the percentage of total profit he expected from each of his three divisions.

In a business plan with written goals, all subdivisions will have clearly defined objectives. They can then sense the degree of their success when looking back and evaluating performance.

When the Harwoods developed their goals for Harwood E&C, the following healthy plan emerged:

1. Achieve 15 percent real growth based on current dollars (compounded to double the *basic* business in five years).
2. Achieve net operating profit (minimum 15 percent of sales) in the coming year.
3. Maintain the family heritage as an aggressive, financially solid, manufacturer of the "HEC trigger," controlling quality and output while creating new, related products through the parent organization and selected subsidiary companies.
4. Maintain a strong family financial position for the

purpose of cooperative accumulation of wealth and internal growth.

5. Beware of acquisitions that require separate facilities and separate management. However, plan to incorporate Dexter Tool Sales, Inc. as a distribution (retail) arm for profit and program development.
6. Develop retail outlets for industrial sales by 1992.
7. Develop a special-purpose service facility on the West Coast to handle business in that area and possibly Pacific markets by 1990.
8. Strengthen overseas expansion with warehousing in Germany, but not until the mark strengthens against the dollar so we can be more competitive. Consider various interim plans to restart growth in German-speaking countries, date pending.
9. Review Canadian manufacturing for long-term profitability and consider reducing our investment and manufacturing involvement by 1990.
10. Explore joint venture in Japan, *if* profitability projections can be supported and *if* it helps ensure growth, by 1990.

These clearly stated goals enabled the Harwoods to implement their program successfully. All family members were in agreement on how and when each goal would be broken down into segments and subsequently sliced up into smaller and smaller increments so it could be explored thoroughly and achieved as all family members envisioned.

A sound business with a thoroughly professionalized management expresses excellence in all its phases. It gets results through the efforts of its participants. In order for all members of the business family to work together, they must first establish basic operating rules. This means they must objectify the process and limit negative or destructive input. The business must feel good to all who are in it.

"No Parking": A Policy on Family Employment

The most common problem that inhibits a family business is employing a relative who is not capable of handling a job professionally or, at the very least, adequately. Sometimes it is lack of skills; more often it is lack of desire or ambition. Competence, not family name, is the key to success. The family business is not a place to "park" relatives; nor is it a social agency. It is an asset held by a family and is probably the biggest asset in the family portfolio.

Therefore, it is important to have a statement of policy on family employment. All family members must adhere to the policy in order for equal employment opportunities to prevail. The following guidelines developed by one business suggest sound criteria for entry:

1. Family members are responsible for expressing appropriate interest in employment opportunities in the company.
2. Family members may not apply for entry-level posts.
3. Family members must have appropriate work experience and fully meet the requirements for the position in order to apply.
4. If possible, family members should not participate in the hiring of other family members.
5. If hired for any position, a family member will be treated the same as anyone else would be in that position.
6. Whenever possible, family members should not directly supervise other family members.
7. Job performance alone will determine advancement, salary reviews, or termination of hired family members.
8. Family members will be paid fair market salaries for jobs performed.

Sound Business Practice

There are five tasks on the way to professionalizing a business.

1. *Examine the family's business management style.* Is it entrepreneurial or is it professional? Since many family businesses began with an enterpreneur, the founder's style may have become standard operating procedure. As the business finds itself on sounder footing, this personalized style will become outdated and inhibit the progress of the business. The successor will find it difficult to imitate what the entrepreneur did naturally.

A continuum of management styles would show a progression from entrepreneurial to professional. The long-range objective in a family enterprise is a well-managed business functioning as far to the professional end as possible. This correlates with the "Fully Achieved" point on the healthy business test. It means the prevailing management techniques will be primarily professional. *The family that fails to recognize and accept the need to move along the continuum will be stuck with a business that functions exactly as the family interacts.*

2. *Identify the family messages.* When interpersonal messages cause problems for the family, the business will be in trouble as well. The family needs to list the messages it broadcasts to its members and determine if any of those messages are in conflict with its business goals. The process begins by identifying the messages stressed by the parents, particularly the entrepreneurial founder. Next, areas of conflict must be located. Of special importance are messages or patterns of behavior that are in conflict with a *healthy business.*

3. *Identify where family members are in their adult development.* Each developmental stage carries with it a specific set of tasks. By the pure nature of their age differences, family members do not operate at the same stage of adult development. Consider a family of three generations: the tasks of the grandson at twenty-six are different from those of the father at fifty-one or the grandfather at seventy-six.

Invariably family members will pass through periods when their developmental tasks are compatible or incompatible. Wherever they are in their stage of development, they must resolve existing conflicts from that point. Only then can the business maintain the stable base it needs to be successful.

Ideas need to be considered on their merit, not on the age or maturity of one family member as seen by another. A family enterprise needs to be run as a business first and then as a vehicle for individual growth.

4. *Recognize how management style, family messages, and stages in adult development affect present business practices and conditions.* Interpersonal problems spilling over in the business may be the root of difficulties that are being blamed on other sources. The best forums for resolving these problems are scheduled family discussions that have specific time limits. The optimum length for such meetings is two hours. Sessions should end at the appointed time, and unfinished topics should be deferred until the next session rather than carried over to the dinner table or the bedroom. To effectively complete this task, family members must communicate openly and directly and be very honest both about themselves and about each other.

5. *Modify or change any behavior that is inhibiting the business from operating professionally.* Some behavior patterns can be changed by technique; others can be changed only by the individuals themselves. Change occurs only when it is sought or desired by the person involved. However, the family that puts forth the honest effort to effect change will reduce the negatives in both business and family life, professionalize the business, and increase profits.

At this point it is helpful to examine your own family business and assess if the tasks described above are being addressed. Such a self-examination helps to clear away the fuzzy thinking that comes from trying to mesh family emotions with business practicalities. Once you uncover your trouble areas, you will need specific techniques to overcome them as you move along the road to professionalizing your business. This is the topic of the following chapter.

12

Professionalizing a Family Business

Some families in business "get stuck" for want of simple techniques to help them progress through the normal decision-making process. There are several tried-and-true methods that can help professionalize your family business. Their simplicity and the fact that they have been universally used does not minimize their value. Here are a few suggestions. Add others as you find them.

See, Record, and Communicate

At all meetings on family business matters, information should be openly recorded and within full view of those attending. A chalkboard works fine for this purpose, but an easel with a flip chart and a magic marker is better. Writing things on a flip chart in a public setting has two benefits. First, everyone can see what is being recorded. Second, written information registers more concretely. People are not always the best listeners.

With verbal communication it is not always possible to establish whether the message being sent is the one being received. With open, written recording, the communication can be checked until all understand it the same way. Written communication also serves as a permanent record of decisions made.

Setting the Agenda

A basic principle in any business is "no surprises." To avoid surprises, a meeting agenda should be agreed upon in advance. Simply asking, "What are the agenda items for our meeting next Tuesday?" will elicit topics. List items on the flip chart along with the name of the person responsible for leading the discussion or preparing the material on that topic.

Any data to be studied in advance should be made available to all parties prior to the meeting. This sounds so reasonable and self-explanatory, but in my experience it is not unusual to hear of a family member who has had an item sprung on him with the directive, "Sign here!" Setting an agenda gives everyone an opportunity to develop it as well as to determine those who will lead the various discussions. Also, giving discussion leaders advance warning prevents them from having to "shoot from the hip." This is in sharp contrast to the family business in which family members stumble into a particular office and start discussing business matters for which they are not prepared. Many families have been caught in brouhahas only to discover that had matters been clarified at the outset, the confusion could have been avoided.

Here is a checklist of criteria for holding a good meeting:

1. Is the purpose of the meeting clear?
2. Does it start promptly and use the allotted time appropriately?

3. Do participants have an opportunity to contribute their ideas and opinions?
4. Are the decisions to be made clearly stated?
5. Are specific action steps outlined with dates for achieving goals?
6. Are specific people assigned responsibility for the actions to be taken?
7. Does everyone agree on when and where to meet next?

This list, I should add, is printed on the back of my business card. Clients tell me they refer to it regularly to keep their meetings focused!

The Fiscal-Year-End Family Meeting

The purpose of the fiscal-year-end family meeting is to educate family members about the enterprise. This meeting is best held informally in the home; once again, it should be scheduled and subject to an established time limit. Concepts such as total percentages, year-end increases, and comparisons with prior years are best conveyed through bar graphs or pie charts. Use of such graphics will help the meeting to stay interesting, make it less verbal, and may even "keep Dad off his soapbox," as one family noted.

Any questions raised in this meeting should be handled like questions in sex education. Give only as much information as is requested rather than reacting off some concern about "telling all the details." Children must be instructed that such "private, family matters" are not to be discussed with anyone outside the family. As the children mature and the parents become more comfortable with this process, greater details will be sought and can be shared.

As I mentioned before, set a time limit for the meeting—a maximum of one hour. Stop at the end of the time allotted.

151

Welcome additional questions when asked, but answer them on a one-on-one basis rather than reconvening as a family. Above all, maintain the family's interest in the meeting and focus on the positive possibilities the future holds. Such a focus will shape the attitudes the children develop about the business.

Brainstorming

Brainstorming has been used for many years to stimulate the production of wide-ranging ideas on a given topic. The basic rule during the first part of the process is "Anything goes." No evaluative comments or judgments are to be made by participants until the brainstorming procedure has stopped.

The purpose of brainstorming is to stimulate people to think of concepts and ideas they might not ordinarily produce. It also unlocks problem-solving groups from being dependent on or dominated by one person. Each person has equal opportunity to offer ideas for consideration; after all, an idea doesn't care who has it. The most dominant person or the one with the loudest voice rarely has all the answers. Brainstorming reduces the proprietary aspects of an idea.

To gain maximum benefit from the brainstorming technique, the following rules should be followed:

1. Define the idea or topic to be brainstormed.
2. Stress that no evaluation or side comments are to be made during the brainstorming process. Any such interruption in the process will reduce the number of ideas stimulated.
3. Have one person act as a scribe and write down on a flip chart all ideas as soon as they are voiced. When no more ideas are vocalized, stop and return to the list.
4. Ask for clarification of each item on the list. The person

who supplied the item is responsible for clarifying it. It is essential to clarify all items on the list.

5. "Reality test" each item with the group. Some items will be off the wall and should be crossed off the list. Others will merit careful consideration.
6. Discuss the ramifications of the items still listed. Ask: "What can be reasonably expected if we did this?" or "Is this realistic?"
7. Set priorities.

If you run into trouble with the brainstorming technique, you may have defined your topic too broadly. When this occurs, redefine the topic, slicing it "thinner." The result will be the generation of more tightly focused ideas.

Setting Priorities

Priorities focus the work to be accomplished by a group. It is conceivable that more than one of the items brainstormed will be a high-priority matter.

The following procedure for setting priorities, like brainstorming itself, minimizes the impact of the loudest voice and makes it possible for all present to cast their ballot.

1. List the items to be considered.
2. Give each person in the group a set of gummed dots. The number of dots depends on the total choices to prioritize, but at least one-third as many dots should be used as there are items listed. For example, if there are eighteen items, each person is given six dots, to distribute over the items as he wishes. More than one dot can be placed on any item.
3. Members take turns placing their dots on the flip chart pad, next to their personal preferences on the list. As

Family Business, Risky Business

the gummed dots are placed on the pad, an immediate profile of the priorities emerges.

A work group should experiment with the number of dots in order to readily achieve clearly separated priorities. If priorities are bunched closely together, the group should be given fewer dots and the process repeated. Once the priorities have been established, each can be discussed in a systematic way and appropriate plans can be formulated.

Outlining Alternatives

Family businesses often do not consider all the alternatives available to them for solving a particular problem. One reason, as mentioned above, is that the loudest or oldest member prevails in decision making. Outlining alternatives opens the floor to discussion and broadens the range of possibilities available. What reasonable person could rationally object to looking at all the alternatives?

The first step in outlining the alternatives is to list them. Again, this can be done by brainstorming. Once the choices are listed, the group can ask, "What can we reasonably expect if we follow alternative 1?" Repeat this question for each alternative and record the reasonable predictions in every case. A reasonable prediction is simply a "best guess." Since none of us can predict the future, each day we take action on our "best guess" at what the future holds. This process simply formalizes reasonable predictions.

When agreement is reached on what can be reasonably predicted for each alternative, review the list and use the priority process again to select a course of action.

Note that this technique reduces ownership of an idea. No longer is it "Dad's brainstorm" or "Linda's suggestion." Diffusing or reducing ownership makes it possible to examine an

154

item more objectively. Comments or criticisms do not get directed personally at the initiator. Thus, ego involvement is less likely to play a role in the decision-making process. Furthermore, the solution will belong to the group with greater commitment to the idea and its implementation.

If no obvious solution emerges from this process, the group should have one of its members study the item further and report back at a future meeting. Also, the group should not overlook doing nothing. This is often a legitimate alternative. However, the process described above usually leads to a preferred choice.

Establishing Criteria for a Decision

Perhaps the most universal operating problem in family-controlled enterprises is the failure to establish criteria for making decisions. Emotional bias or tunnel vision guides the decision where cool, reasoned judgment should prevail.

Also, groups may jump to a solution and begin mapping an implementation plan *before* reaching agreement on the criteria that will be used to make the decision. *Establish the criteria for making the decision first.* The rest is simple.

Assume, for example, that a family business needs a new controller. Various family members propose candidates for the position, some of whom are present. The family then begins to discuss the people named. But they have not determined any criteria for a controller. When the criteria are finally set down, none of the candidates is qualified. Family members simply polarize around their favorite candidates and begin to argue for each person's preferred choice. Establishing, then applying, criteria can avert a family fight.

Written job descriptions are an excellent example of establishing criteria in advance of a specific decision. In the above situation, a great deal of time and energy would have been saved if the family had prepared a list of requirements for the position of controller—in effect, a job description.

In the decision-making process, criteria are much less volatile than solutions or candidates proposed. It is easier to discuss and debate criteria because people have much less invested in them personally. Somehow our egos are closely identified with our ideas and proposals. Any procedure that reduces ego identification will lead to a more objective examination of the item under consideration. Once established, the criteria often make the choice of alternatives obvious.

Once again, the objectivity of this process depersonalizes decision making and defuses potentially volatile matters within the group. It also tends to reduce the force of the loudest voice or the person most dominant for whatever reason. The loudest voices rarely have the best solutions for everything.

To order the importance of individual criteria, it is useful again to employ the gummed dots, this time using different colors to indicate value:

Red = Must have; critical
Yellow = Nice to have but not absolutely essential
Green = Pure gravy, a bonus

List all potential criteria. Then prioritize them by placing the colored dots above the criteria. (The group may want to experiment with the number of colored dots. Too many will produce too many "must have" criteria; too few will have the opposite effect.)

When decision making becomes easier with much less "heat," ego involvement, or personal advocacy, the quality of the decisions will improve.

The Four-Plus-One Method

Research into the effectiveness of groups and the quality of their decision making has uncovered some interesting facts.

Compare the results of two work groups. One group consists of five people, all of whom are knowledgeable about the problem under consideration. It will produce an acceptable solution. Another group of five has four people who are knowledgeable and one who is not. The group of four plus one will consistently produce superior, more creative solutions than the group of five experts. This occurs because the non-knowledgeable person makes comments that precipitate more thorough examination of the issue. These comments might take the form of "Why do you do it that way?" or "I don't understand how that solution will be best." They force the group to take a closer look at the alternatives before choosing one as a solution.

If questions like those raised in the four-plus-one situation are not acceptable within the family group—typically because one member always dominates—then that family is not taking full advantage of all the human resources within its system. Such a family needs to gain access to all the talent it has available. This can be accomplished by using the techniques I have described for defusing both ego involvement and ownership of ideas.

Handling Conflict

In working through the tasks described in this chapter, a family can expect to have periods of conflict. The various "tools, gizmos, and gadgets" offered will focus the work group on the issue and eliminate many of the problems otherwise encountered. However, conflict is normal and healthy and needs to be managed.

In a healthy business, high conflict or clash over tasks and projects is normal. Relatively little energy is spent clashing over interpersonal difficulties because sufficient energy has been devoted to working those through. The parties can then stand toe to toe, debate issues, and work them through to a solution. Then, each person can walk away respecting the others because of or in spite of the transaction itself.

Many of the conflict issues in a family business relate to self-image. Each person has an ideal self-image developed over many years through contact with family members and other significant people. The actual self-image is revealed in the behavior a person manifests as a result of experiences and feedback received from all those around him. A person will be most comfortable when the actual self-image and the ideal self-image overlap sufficiently. When there is a separation between the ideal and the actual self-image, the discomfort can escalate to frustration and anger, as shown in Figure 8.

The discomfort, frustration, and anger are translated into psychic pain in the individual's mind. The normal response to pain is aggression. Behavior that stems from a base of aggression is unstable and erratic. Psychic pain that is inwardly directed is expressed as passive aggression; it leads to confusion and missed opportunities because the person internalizes the aggression. Ultimately it results in depression. Psychic pain that is outwardly directed is expressed as active aggression; it alienates others, and the individual comes off as an angry person. Neither active nor passive aggression addresses the source of the discomfort, which is the separation of the images. Either extreme pulls the business down.

Solving this problem means addressing its source. Either the ideal image must be scaled down or modified so that it and the actual image can overlap or the actual behavior must change to become more in keeping with the ideal. While it is true that a person can do anything he wishes to do, it is important that the desire for that goal emanate from the person himself.

Throughout life the overlap position between the ideal and the actual self-image fluctuates. A healthy person recognizes this and makes the necessary behavior modifications to stay in the comfort zone.

Figure 8. The effects of separation between ideal self-image and actual self-image.

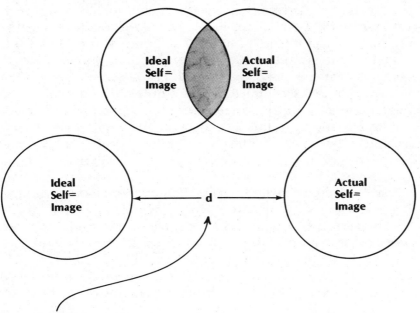

Separation of the ideal and actual images leads to:

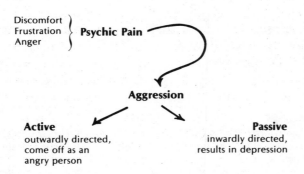

Neither active nor passive aggression addresses the source of the discomfort which is the separation of images.

Family Business, Risky Business

In a business conflict situation, if the interpersonal issues are not resolved, the self-image comes into play. For example, at a meeting Joe presents an idea that he thinks is fine. Mary responds with "What a lousy idea!" This precipitates a separation in Joe's self-image. A healthy solution is to examine the content of the issue to see whether or not it *is* a lousy idea. If Joe finds that this is so, he can modify his ideal notion and move back into the comfort zone. An unhealthy solution is for Joe to become so uncomfortable with the separation of images that he gets angry. At this display of outward aggression, Mary becomes passive and withdraws. Nothing is solved. No one can move to a decision, and the issue's continuance leads to further conflict.

At the opposite extreme is the failure to deliver a message that is in any way negative. The downfall of many family enterprises is the inability of key actors to confront one another over crucial matters. The ideal self-image of the family in this situation is not to confront. To do so is unconscionable. In such a case, the entire family must change behavior and adopt a new ideal image that permits confrontation if the business is to succeed.*

Countless families have failed in their business efforts because they did not identify the problems that faced them. They played hit and miss with those skills and techniques that pull a business together without tearing a family apart. The information and technological explosion of this past century makes it increasingly necessary to include more people in the decision-making process. In government and corporate business, decisions are the result of wide-ranging discussions from

---

*A look at the roots of the word *confront* is useful. According to the *Random House Dictionary of English Usage, con* stands for "connection; together" and *front* signifies "a place or position directly before anything." Thinking of confrontation as connecting with an issue and bringing it to the forefront for consideration is a much more positive approach than viewing it as an adversarial transaction.

many sources. Who actually pronounces the decision is often pro forma matter.

Family business experiences additional stress under these condition. Decisions are at the mercy of communications technology, and there is no time to allow matters to evolve naturally. Families with unresolved personal issues cannot function effectively in a situation that demands immediate attention without personal priorities influencing the outcome. It is, therefore, more important than ever—in fact, the key to survival—for the family business to professionalize itself as quickly as possible. The techniques outlined in this chapter will go a long way toward doing this.

After the business arm of the family is in order, the family can turn its attention to the messages it wants to express. Quality and excellence never go out of style. The family that professionalizes its business operation achieves both. Along the way, it learns the skills that enhance its vitality as a unique unit. A family tradition can be built in an atmosphere of mutual trust and respect along with the special caring that family members extend to each other. Profits are gained at all levels.

Epilogue

Three cheers for family business! Without the courageous entrepreneurs and the families who have carried out that vision, American enterprise would not be where it is today. More than 90 percent of all businesses in the United States are family held and controlled. Their philosophies embody the American commercial spirit.

In recent years employment in the Fortune 500 companies reached a peak. But job opportunities continued to grow. It was small businesses and family-held businesses that took up the slack and thus provided a continuously strong environment for American workers. At the same time, men and women ages twenty to thirty-five were developing technology to new highs, especially in the computer field. From the special effects in the films of Steven Spielberg and George Lucas to the Apple™ in the classroom, to the Atari™ in the game room, and to the computerized assembly line, a young generation of entrepreneurs has moved America into the twenty-first century.

As these new entrepreneurs negotiate the shoals of family-operated or closely held businesses, certain problems are bound to arise. But unlike previous generations, they need not bind themselves into situations that destroy what vision has built.

The four core tasks examined in this book will keep these

young entrepreneurs from the pitfalls of the past and disengage established family businesses from negative patterns. Because they are so important, let's review them again:

1. Develop the family genogram and identify the family's behavioral messages.
2. Understand how these messages affect the business operation and/or contradict sound business practice.
3. Modify the family behavioral functions to minimize the negative impact of these actions on the family's business arm.
4. Move the business to a professional level while being certain to use the skills and talents of *all* family members who wish to be involved. This is what makes the family business unique.

Once good communication is established among family members, problems can be solved. After all, every problem has a solution on its other side. The satisfaction that comes from solving problems together is a strong step in binding the family together. It builds the confidence and trust that are the glue of relationships. Also, family members begin to feel good about themselves. It is a joy to work in this positive atmosphere. For a family's customers and clients, it is a great place to do business.

When these four tasks are accomplished, no family business ever needs to fear its dissolution from the pitfalls that entrapped families in other historical eras. Just as American society has used technology to attain a new level of understanding the world, so family businesses need to find techniques that will help them understand their true worth to the capitalist system.

Family business built the American dream. It can not only keep it alive but expand it beyond its own vision. Somewhere in America today is a young entrepreneur who has built a better mousetrap and is busy selling it to satisfy his vision. Likely, his wife is the marketing director, his daughter heads production, and his son balances the books. The company has a nursery for the younger children, and the employees play volleyball at lunch for fitness.

Down the road is an established family business with a new president. The daughter of the founder has taken the reins of a prosperous family enterprise. She has a vision of her own and starts out to reinvent the family wheel. But before she can do that, she has to attend to the problems generated by years of little communication among family members.

Both Mr. Mousetrap and Founder's Daughter must accomplish the same four tasks if they are to succeed in gaining not only profits but family unity. They must take their clues not from the sensationalized dramas of TV and books—whether fiction of nonfiction—but from a combination of communications and family systems theory, shored up by the tenets of sound business practice.

The day that family businesses close their doors and entrepreneurs are discouraged from their visionary pursuits will mark not only the fall of capitalism in America but the passing of a spirit and a dream that has served us well. To keep that from happening, all members of family businesses, both established and emerging, must see themselves in a clear light. It is far from an impossible task.

As I travel America in my professional career and see what family business has brought forth and continues to generate, my faith in the capacity of our national genius is ever renewed. It is my "vision" that this book will help family members generate and/or renew their own hopes and dreams in the prize they hold and share, the family business.

Appendix
What to Do When Your Family in Business Needs Help

Locating a Consultant

There are consultants throughout the United States who can be helpful to families in business. Here is a procedure for selecting a consultant, starting first in your own community.

The first hurdle to overcome in seeking help is your own resistance to sharing information about your business. It is not unusual for families to be reluctant to talk about their businesses with "outsiders." The underlying issue is trust. If you trust the professional with whom you are working, then you will freely share information. To reach that level of trust requires effort and a willingness to take risks.

Start by discussing your concerns with those advisors you

already know. Try your banker, accountant, attorney, physician, the head of your local Chamber of Commerce, the head of your trade association, or some other person in business whom you respect. You may be surprised how willing people are to help. Use the "networking" principle. Provide the person with enough details so that he understands the problem. Make it clear that you are not asking him for the solution but recognize that he may be able to assist. Then ask, "Whom do you know that might be helpful in finding a solution?" Many people throw up their hands when they hear about problems in family business so don't be discouraged if that happens. Your goal is to expand your network and make contact with someone who can assist you. When you think you have found someone, there are a series of questions to ask and facts to establish.

As you know from having read this book, I am partial to the systems approach to family business. If your concern in any way relates to family or interpersonal relationships, then a consultant who has a solid understanding of family systems will be invaluable in helping to find a solution. However, that alone is not enough; business knowledge and acumen on the part of your consultant are also essential.

When you locate a consultant who possesses this combination, arrange for an interview. Ask for references of people with whom he has worked. Prior to the interview, contact the references.

Here are some questions you might ask during a reference check:

> What was the nature of the problem that prompted the person to call the consultant?
> How did the consultant go about helping to find an acceptable solution?
> Did the consultant manage the relationship in a satisfactory manner?

Appendix

Did the consultant understand the special conditions
found in family business?
If the person were to do it all over again, would he proceed
in the same way?
Was the consultant a good listener, and did he really grasp
the problem in its entirety?
Was he satisfied with the final outcome?
What recommendations does he have for making the best
use of the consultant's talents and skills?

After you have gathered this information from the referral
sources, you are ready to interview the consultant. In the
interview, present your problem as candidly and succinctly as
possible, and then ask the candidate how he or she would
approach it. Listen carefully to the answer and pay close
attention to how you *feel* during the exchange. If you are
satisfied with the answers to your questions and feel positive
about the exchange—and if the data from the referral sources
was satisfactory—then there is a good chance that you have
found the right person.

The best solutions to your problems will be those you are
directly involved in developing. Think of it as an educational
process, of learning how to help yourself. There is no "quick
fix" for most things so beware of those who suggest otherwise.
It takes a long time for most situations to evolve and changes
are not made overnight.

Self-Help for the Family Business

There are a limited number of self-help groups—people in
family businesses who have banded together to assist one
another. Listed below are addresses and names of contacts
current as of this writing:

Arizona   Arizona Family Business Council
c/o Mr. Robert Huntington, Jr.
Huntington Valley Seed Company
1918 Van Buren
Phoenix, Arizona 85001

Chicago   Chicago Family Business Council
Robert Render, President
327 S. LaSalle Street, Suite 1700
Chicago, Illinois 60604

Minnesota Minnesota Family Business Council
Marty Kupper, President
P.O. Box 35133
Minneapolis, Minnesota 55435

I would appreciate learning about other self-help groups. Please send information to:

David Bork
Coda Corporation
7236 Ridge Road
Frederick, Maryland 21701

Notes

Chapter 1

1. Pamela G. Hollie, "On 7th Avenue, It's All in the Family," *The New York Times*, June 26, 1983.
2. Jane Freundel Levey, "When a Kiss Turns 'Daddy's Girl' into His Professional Partner," *The Washington Post*, March 4, 1984, Section C-3.
3. Gary Pomerantz, "Two Cookes Are Not Too Many," *The Washington Post*, February 23, 1984, Section D. On March 1, 1985, the *Post* reported that Jack Kent Cooke had purchased the outstanding stock in the Redskins from long-time owner Edward Bennett Williams, who stepped down as president of the organization. Whether or not John Kent Cooke will assume that title was unknown at the time this book was written.
4. Paul Taylor, "Washing the Blues Away," *The Washington Post*, November 23, 1984, Section A-3.

Chapter 3

1. Murray Bowen, *Family Therapy in Clinical Practice* (New York: J. Aronson, 1978).
2. Walter Toman, *Family Constellation* (New York: Springer Publishing Co., 1976).

3. G. B. Stern, *The Matriarch,* 1925 reprint (San Diego: Pyramid Publishing Co., 1967).
4. Eleanor Estes, *The Middle Moffat* (New York: Hargreaves Publishing Co., 1979).
5. Donald A. Price, "Adler, Toman, and Bowen: Family Constellations and Projection Process in Personality Development," *The Family,* Volume 7, No. 2, p. 79.
6. Cecile Ernst and Jules Angst, *Birth Order and Its Influence on Personality* (New York: Springer-Verlag, 1983).

Chapter 9

1. Joanna Biggar, "The Biz Kids," *The Washington Post Magazine,* January 20, 1985.

Chapter 10

1. "The Bass Dynasty," *Newsweek,* November 19, 1984, pp. 72–81.

Chapter 11

1. David P. Campbell, *If You Don't Know Where You're Going, You'll Probably End Up Somewhere Else* (Niles, Ill.: Argus Communications, 1974).

For Further Reading

All the books listed in this section are highly recommended reading. Taken as a unit, they represent the view that people are important and that the quality of a product or procedure has never gone out of style. I've included a few words about each one.

Books on Management and Business Practice

Blanchard, Kenneth, and Spencer Johnson, *The One Minute Manager*. William Morrow and Company, 1981, 111 pages.

On the surface, this book is deceptively simple. It is based on sound theories about motivation. The prevailing tone is the win-win approach to managing people. Plain and simple: It works!

Fisher, Roger, and William Ury, *Getting to Yes: Negotiating Agreement Without Giving In*. Houghton Mifflin, 1981, 163 pages.

Success in any business is measured by profits produced

by people who feel good about their work. Creating a win-win environment where all parties feel positive about their contributions is the benchmark of a soundly managed company. Employees who maximize their contributions while simultaneously feeling good about them create a win-win environment. Fisher and Ury have done an excellent job of describing a process that helps to create a positive environment for employing people.

Gardner, John W., *Excellence*. Harper & Row, 1961, 161 pages.

This book has long been a favorite and rightly so. John Gardner examines the entire range of contributions to society, whether it be from the excellence of scholars or the excellence of tradesmen. It contains his famous quote: "We must pay attention to the quality of our philosophies and the quality of our plumbing, for if we do not, then neither our philosophies nor our pipes will hold water."

Peters, Thomas J., and Robert H. Waterman, Jr., *In Search of Excellence*. Harper & Row, 1982, 360 pages.

This book has captured the public market, with more than 1,300,000 copies sold. Drawing from extensive surveys of companies on the American scene, the authors have extrapolated a series of key points that characterize the best-run companies. Any enterprise that keeps these salient points foremost in mind will move a long way toward achieving results.

Schumacher, E. F., *Small Is Beautiful*. Harper & Row, 1973, 305 pages.

Part of the American ethos is the notion that the West is waiting there to be conquered, and if a little bit of something is good, then a lot more is better. That view leads some businesspeople to think in terms of growth and expansion as the only answer for their enterprise. Schumacher takes an antithetical point of view. He says not necessarily that small *is* better but rather that people should consider all the alternatives available, then elect a course of action that satisfies their own priorities. Growth for its own sake is not always beneficial.

Sloma, Richard S., *No-Nonsense Management: A General Manager's Primer.* Macmillan, 1977, 157 pages.

Most people in business are very pragmatic. More than one owner of a family business has said to me, "Don't confuse me with the theories; just tell me what will work." This book contains 157 pages and 70 chapters. Sometimes the entire message of the chapter can be found in its title. Examples:

- An effective general manager is an expert juggler.
- Be known to have ambition; never be known as ambitious.
- The "BS" content in a firm's communications system is proportional to the number of layers in the organization.
- There are really only two types of problems: growth problems and liquidation problems. Growth problems are better.

Other Important Books

Some of the most satisfied people in business are those who have well-integrated personalities and have a very clear picture of themselves. The following books address the task of becoming well integrated.

Bolles, Richard Nelson, *What Color Is Your Parachute?* Ten Speed Press, 1972, 293 pages.

This consistent best seller has helped people think through the options they have in life. It presents a systematic method for looking at careers and jobs as well as giving very sound advice about how to proceed. Sometimes the members of a family business need to know their other options. The book is now being revised each year to incorporate ideas sent to the author by his readers.

Campbell, David P., *If You Don't Know Where You're Going, You'll Probably End Up Somewhere Else.* Argus Communications, 1974, 144 pages.

This is a dandy little book about goals, objectives, and finding one's way in life. The language is geared for a teenager, but the message is no less valid for people of all ages. This can be useful with young people in getting them to look at the opportunities that exist within their own environment.

Levinson, Daniel J., with Charlotte N. Darrow, Edward B. Klein, Maria H. Levinson, and Braxton McKee. *The Seasons of a Man's Life.* Alfred A. Knopf, 1978, 363 pages.

Many writers have discussed the predictable stages of adult development, with the bulk of the research focused on men. This book points out the differences in the various developmental tasks, with the hope that parallel data will soon be available for women.

Peck, M. Scott, *The Road Less Traveled: A New Psychology of Love, Traditional Values, and Spiritual Growth.* Simon & Schuster, 1978, 316 pages.

While readers may not agree with every point presented by Peck, a working knowledge of concepts within this book will take them a long way toward being well-integrated people. The section about love is the best I have seen on the subject.

For Further Reading

Toman, Walter, *Family Constellation*. Springer Publishing Company, 1976, 333 pages.

One must take all the research about birth position with a grain of salt since there are so many extenuating circumstances that would change the interpretation. In fact, it is probably fair to say that use of birth order information is more of an art than a science since in no way can it be viewed as empirical. At the same time, it can be a very useful tool in gaining insight into patterns of behavior in a business. Readers are cautioned not to be dogmatic in their application of these theories or, for that matter, any theories about human behavior, because there are always exceptional circumstances.

Some writers have attempted to discredit all the birth order studies. Careful examination of these efforts will reveal that the detractors have been less than thorough in making a one-to-one correlation between the material they wish to discredit and the studies they use for that purpose.

Vaillant, George E., *Adaptation to Life: How the Best and the Brightest Came of Age*. Little, Brown and Company, 1977, 396 pages.

In 1937, the W. T. Grant Foundation underwrote a study of adult development. A selection of freshmen entering Harvard were tested and interviewed, as were their parents. In a 25-year longitudinal study, these people were interviewed and asked to complete questionnaires. While there is a lot about this study to criticize—i.e., all-male sample, children of opportunity, very waspish, all white—it is the only research of its kind.

The study groups the respondents into three categories: most successful, successful, and least successful. Success is not defined so much in terms of salary earned but by such factors as increased levels of responsibility, sustained performance, and effectiveness of relationships. Often people in family-controlled businesses have no basis for comparing themselves with the larger world since they have spent all their working lives within the family-held enterprise.

I often give clients an annotated copy of this book, so they can see themselves in the larger continuum. This is a way of reinforcing the most successful people in a family-held business.

Index

Index

Grant, Alan, father-daughter team of, 6

Grant, Leslie, on cooperation and communication, 6

Great Depression, 3

Green, Henrietta Howland Robinson, career of, 3, 126

Hallmark, women managers in, 69

Hancock, John, as entrepreneur, 1-2

Hancock, Thomas, as entrepreneur, 1

Hazen, Freddie, on success of family business, 6

Healthy Business Test, purpose and elements of, 138-139, 140-141

heirs:
  inactive, 129-130
  individual, 125-126
  multiple, 127-129
  widows, 130-131

Honig, Leo, on family relationships in business, 6

If You Don't Know Where You're Going, You'll Probably End Up Somewhere Else (Campbell), 139

inactive family heirs, settlement with, 129-130

individuation, *see* differentiation of self

in-law(s), 81-88
  conflict resolution by, 87-88

family messages and, 86-87

job description criteria for, 82

problems caused by, 81-87

training of, 81-82

job descriptions, importance of, 155-156

Jung, Carl, individuation theory of, 32

lose-lose strategies, elements of, 52

McCormick, Cyrus, as entrepreneur, 3

management styles, entrepreneurial versus professional, 145
  see also professional management techniques

Matriarch, The (Stern), 37

meetings, 149-151
  agenda setting for, 150-151
  communication techniques for, 149-150
  criteria checklist for, 150-151
  at fiscal year end, 151-152
  time limits for, 151

Men's Apparel Forum, training offered by, 123

mentoring, nature and value of, 115-116

message chart, *see* family message chart

Middle Moffat, The (Estes), 37-38

Morgan, J. Pierpont, as entrepreneur, 3

Index

women in business
   as entrepreneurs, 56, 59, 84-87
   in father-daughter ventures, 6
   as heirs, 126
   number of, 69-70
   problems of, 78-79
   stereotyping of, 18-21, 78-79
   traditional view of, 70

in twentieth century, 5
unequal compensation of,
   78-79
wife's role and, 11, 12-13,
   72-73, 76-78
see also daughters
World War II, business growth
   during, 4